Edith Kellnhauser

Fachenglisch für Pflegekräfte

Edith Kellnhauser

Fachenglisch für Pflegekräfte

Die Nutzung englischer Fachtermini am Beispiel der Pflege in den USA

schlütersche

Bibliografische Information Der Deutschen Bibliothek
Die Deutsche Bibliothek verzeichnet diese Publikation in der Deutschen Nationalbibliografie; detaillierte bibliografische Daten sind im Internet über http://dnb.ddb.de abrufbar.

ISBN 3-87706-898-7

Anschrift der Autorin:

Dr. phil. Edith Kellnhauser
Friedrichstraße 44
55124 Mainz

Edith Kellnhauser hat Jahrzehnte in den USA als Krankenschwester und im Pflegemanagement gearbeitet. Bis 1999 war sie Professorin für Pflegewissenschaft/Pflegemanagement an der Katholischen Fachhochschule in Mainz und baute als Gründungsdekanin die neuen Pflegestudiengänge mit auf. Sie ist Autorin bzw. Herausgeberin zahlreicher pflegefachlicher Publikationen.

Gestaltung: Schlütersche GmbH & Co. KG, Verlag und Druckerei, Hannover
Satz: PER Digitaler Workflow GmbH, Braunschweig
Druck und Bindung: Druckhaus „Thomas Müntzer“ GmbH, Bad Langensalza

Inhalt / Contents

Entstehungsgeschichte

Die Idee zu diesem Buch ist während meiner mehrjährigen Vorlesungen zum Thema »Englische Fachterminologie« an der Katholischen Fachhochschule in Mainz entstanden. Dabei konnte ich das vorhandene Wissen, aber auch die bestehenden Lücken der Studierenden in der anglo-amerikanischen Fachsprache erkennen. Gefehlt hat mir dabei ein Buch, das die Termini des beruflichen Umfeldes und des pflegerischen Alltags im Zusammenhang mit den praktizierten Arbeitsmethoden speziell in den USA behandelt. So war ich gezwungen, zum einen das von mir aus dortigen Krankenhäusern mitgebrachte Schriftgut zu verwenden und mir zum anderen entsprechende Unterlagen von meinen Kolleginnen aus USA schicken zu lassen. Durch diese Notlösung konnte zu den einzelnen Themen jeweils einschlägiges Schriftmaterial verteilt und genutzt werden.

In den Jahren meiner Lehrtätigkeit sind in der Zeit des Grundstudiums zirka 15 % der Studierenden aus Mainz für eine 4-wöchige Hospitation in die USA gereist. Dabei hat sich gezeigt, dass es für einen optimalen Erfolg eines solchen Praktikums sehr wichtig ist, entsprechende fachsprachliche Vorbereitungen durchzuführen.

Dieses Buch soll die bestehenden fachsprachlichen Lücken schließen helfen und es soll allen interessierten Pflegestudentinnen die diesbezüglichen Vorbereitungen auf eine Hospitation in den USA erleichtern.

Nebenbei bemerkt profitieren davon nicht nur die Studierenden, die in die USA reisen, sondern aufgrund der sehr ähnlichen Terminologie auch alle Studierenden, die in andere englisch sprechende Länder gehen.

Abstract

In diesem Buch wird zunächst auf die Art der formalen Vorbereitungen eingegangen, die für einen Aufenthalt von Pflegepersonen in den USA erforderlich sind. Als Einstieg in den Themenbereich wird das amerikanische Gesundheitssystem vorgestellt. Als ein Aspekt dieses Systems wird beispielhaft der Betrieb eines Krankenhauses aufgezeigt. Als Teilbereich eines Krankenhauses wird die Abteilung des Pflegedienstes aus unterschiedlichen Perspektiven beleuchtet. Im Zusammenhang damit werden die strukturellen Gegebenheiten sowie die methodischen Vorgehensweisen bei der Arbeit auf einer Pflegestation verdeutlicht. Im Anschluss daran werden die beruflichen Voraussetzungen zur Anstellung, die Arbeitsanforderungen sowie Vergütungen und Vergünstigungen erläutert. Schließlich werden die unterschiedlichen Möglichkeiten zur pflegerischen Ausbildung sowie bestimmte Ausbildungsinhalte beispielhaft vorgestellt.

Der Text ist bewusst größtenteils in englisch verfasst. Dies soll die Leserinnen befähigen, sich in die englische Satzstellung und in das sinngemäße Verständnis bestimmter Termini hineinzufinden. Dadurch werden sie feststellen, dass eine wörtliche Übersetzung von Begriffen ohne kontextuellen Zusammenhang meist wenig Sinn ergibt oder zu einer falschen Interpretation führt.

Als Lesehilfe werden jeweils im unteren Teil jeder Seite bestimmte im Text vorkommende (wahrscheinlich unbekannte) englische Worte ins Deutsche übersetzt. Die Auswahl dieser Worte basiert auf meinen Lehrerfahrungen mit den Englischkenntnissen von Studierenden im Fach »Englische Fachterminologie«. Die Lesehilfe kann von den Leserinnen auch als Selbsttest genutzt werden, indem sie den englischen Text lesen und im Abgleich mit der Übersetzung ihren Grad des Verständnisses prüfen.

Zielgruppe

Das Buch richtet sich hauptsächlich an Krankenschwestern und Krankenpfleger, die in den USA in einem Krankenhaus hospitieren, einen beruflichen Informationsbesuch durchführen oder dort arbeiten möchten. Deshalb liegt der inhaltliche Schwerpunkt auf der Darstellung bestimmter beruflicher Arbeitsabläufe und deren arbeitstheoretischen Zusammenhängen im Hospital.

Außerdem soll das Buch jenen Studierenden hilfreich sein, für die das Lesen englischer Pflegeliteratur eine Pflichtübung ist und/oder deren Vorlesungen teilweise in englischer (Fach-)Sprache stattfinden.

Lehrenden in den Hochschulen sowie in den Krankenpflegeschulen soll durch die Übersetzung zahlreicher Fachtermini die Lektüre von anglo-amerikanischen Fachbüchern und -artikeln erleichtert und zusammenhängend damit Einblicke in den beruflichen Hintergrund amerikansicher Pflege vermitteln werden. Zum Verständnis dafür, wie dieser Hintergrund durch die berufliche Ausbildung beeinflusst und bestimmt wird, werden gewisse Aspekte der Ausbildung beleuchtet.

Leitenden Personen in der Pflege soll dieses Buch dienlich sein bei ihrer Vorbereitung auf bestimmte Managementaspekte fixierte Informationsbesuche in den USA. Das Aufzeigen der dort bestehenden gesundheitsbehördlichen Vorschriften, der beruflichen Arbeitsstrukturen- und methoden soll das Verstehen des Erlebten vor Ort erleichtern und erweitern.

1 The Preparations for going to the USA

In diesem Kapitel werden die notwendigen Vorbereitungen für einen beruflichen Aufenthalt in den USA aufgezeigt. Eingeteilt nach zwei verschiedenen Zielen eines derartigen Aufenthalts werden entsprechend zwei unterschiedliche Wege erläutert. Speziell der Erwerb einer für einen Arbeitsaufenthalt erforderlichen beruflichen Lizenz durch Absolvieren bestimmter Examina wird verdeutlicht. Es werden Hinweise und Tipps sowohl für die Beschaffung eines Hospitationsplatzes als auch für einen Arbeitsplatz gegeben.

1.1 Different ways to get to the United States

For a professional stay in the United States there are different ways in which this can be accomplished. Following, two such ways are described.

- The first way is **not to work** there professionally,
- The second way is **to work** there professionally.

1.1.1 The First Way

The first way is chosen by persons who do **not want to work** professionally in the United States but want to observe certain aspects of American nursing, nursing management, nursing education or other nursing areas. They want to do a period of observation or an internship.

These persons do not intend to work as a nurse. This is good so, because the German nursing certificates are not accepted in the United States and therefore these persons are not allowed to work in their professional capacity. The duration of their stay is self-limited, usually 4–6 weeks or less. This way is usually taken by nurses alongside of their regular employment in Germany or during their vacation, or by nurse students during their semester break.

1.1.1.1 A Place for an Internship

In order to obtain a place for an internship you can inform yourself via the internet about health care institutions and/or nursing education in colleges and universities. Another way is to utilize the experience of German nursing students at universities of applied sciences and universities who have done internships in the United States.

to accomplish – erreichen, **to observe** – beobachten, **internship** – Praktikum, **nursing certificates** – pflegerische Staatsexamen, **professional capacity** – berufliche Funktion, **duration** – Zeitraum, **self-limited** – selbst beschränkt, **alongside** – neben, **employment** – Anstellung, **vacation** – Urlaub, **semester break** – Semesterferien, **to obtain** – erwerben, **experience** – Erfahrung, **university of applied sciences** – Fachhochschule

1.1.1.2 The Letter of Application

After you have chosen a place for your internship, generally a letter of application is sent to a certain person in the particular facility. Two points in this letter are crucial for the success expected. **Firstly,** the letter should be addressed in name to a certain person in that institution. **Do not use** the unspecific terms: Dear Sir, Dear Madam, Gentlemen. If you do this your letter is likely to wander through several departments in a large institution and may never reach its intended destination. And you wonder why you do not get an answer.

Secondly, make sure you use the proper terminology for the purpose of your stay. Remember, you want to **observe,** gather **information, do an internship.** Since on account of professional regulations you are not allowed to work as a nurse you **do not use** the words work, practice, practical work, practice time. These words can be misunderstood and as a result can produce a negative answer to your application.

Furthermore, you want to observe and gather information about **certain aspects** in nursing. What in particular are you interested in? Since designated persons in the institution you are going to are preparing an agenda for the total time of your stay they need to know in advance where to place you during what time. Therefore, **do** state in your letter the areas or aspects of your specific interest. For instance, in the management area you are interested in:

- the management of nursing care, use of nursing theories,
- the practice of primary nursing,
- the effects of quality assurance on patients, staff and the organization,
- the use of computer technologiy in nursing,
- the staff performance appraisal,
- the career ladder program,
- the staff development in-house education, continuing education,
- and others of your choice.

For instance, in the educational area you are interested in:

- the curriculum of the basic nursing education program,
- the coordination of theoretical teaching and practical instruction,
- the financial support of the students,
- the criteria for student admission to the program,

application – Bewerbung, **particular facility** – bestimmte Einrichtung, **crucial** – entscheidend, **success expected** – erwarteter Erfolg, **addressed in name** – namentlich adressiert, **unspecific terms** – allgemeine Anreden, **intended destination** – beabsichtigtes Ziel, **proper terminology** – richtige Wortwahl, **purpose** – Absicht, **to gather** – sammeln, **on account of professional regulations** – aufgrund professioneller Vorschriften, **result** – Ergebnis, **to produce** – erzeugen, **furthermore** – des Weiteren, **in particular** – speziell, **designated** – beauftragt, **to prepare in advance** – im vorhinein vorbereiten, **to state** – angeben, **area** – Bereich, **effects** – Auswirkungen, **staff performance appraisal** – Mitarbeiterbewertung, **career ladder** – Karriereleiter, **staff development** – Mitarbeiterentwicklung, **in-house education** – innerbetriebliche Fortbildung, **continuing education** – regelmäßige Fortbildung, **support** – Unterstützung

- the financing of the study program,
- the job description for a lecturer/professor,
- the job description for a tutor/mentor,
- and others of your choice.

Finally, the inclusion of a letter of recommendation from your superior at your place of work or from a professor at your place of study with your application creates a favorable impression on the reader and may enhance your chances for acceptance.

1.1.1.3 Visa

For a short stay up to 90 days you do not need a visa. You can simply travel on your German passport which must still be valid for 6 months counting from the day of entry into the United States (American Consulate Frankfurt am Main 2002).

1.1.1.4 Language

In order for you to benefit the most from your stay in the USA you should refresh your English language capabilities prior to departure. A course in specific nursing and health terminology will be especially helpful.

1.1.2 The Second Way

The second way is chosen by persons who **want to work** professionally in the United States. These persons are Krankenschwestern und Krankenpfleger in Germany but do not have a professional license to practice nursing in the United States. This means they are not RNs = registered nurses in the United States. A professional license to work as a registered nurse in the United States is issued by the State Board of Nursing (see chapter 4, quality patient care). To obtain a professional nursing license the following steps have to be taken.

1.1.2.1 Licensure

An applicant has to pass the so called CGFNS examination – Commission on Graduates of Foreign Nursing Schools. This examination is held several times per year in the Amerika Haus in Frankfurt am Main. The system of examination is multiple choice questions from all areas of nursing. A thorough knowledge in all areas of nursing, as well as a good knowledge of English is required to pass the exam. In case of failure the test can be repeated at another time.

job description – Tätigkeitsbeschreibung, **letter of recommendation** – Empfehlungsschreiben, **superior** – Vorgesetzter, **creates a favorable impression** – bewirkt einen günstigen Eindruck, **enhance** – erhöhen, **acceptance** – Annahme, **valid** – gültig, **entry** – Eintritt, **to benefit** – profitieren, **capabilities** – Fähigkeiten, **prior to departure** – vor Abreise, **licence** – Lizenz, **State Board of Nursing** – Pflegekammer, **applicant** – Antragsteller, **to pass** – bestehen, **area** – Gebiet, **thorough knowledge** – gündliche Kenntnisse, **to require** – fordern, **failure** – Nichtbestehen, **to repeat** – vorbereiten

To prepare for the examination information can be obtained from the Council of International Educational Exchange e.V. in Frankfurt (address see appendix). Part of the information package sent to you is a small booklet called *Path to CGFNS Certification – Applicant Handbook*. It contains all necessary information about the obtainment of licensure. In addition, a list of books and tapes helpful for preparing for the exam is part of the package. Most important for preparing for the exam is the book called *Official Study Guide for the CGFNS Qualifying Exam, 4th Edition,* which can be purchased directly from the Commission in Philadelphia (address see appendix).
Note: The CGFNS examination is required by the majority of states in the United States. Each state has its own State Board of Nursing, which establishes the requirements for foreign educated nurses in their state (CGFNS 2002). This means before preparations for taking the CGFNS examination are initiated it is worth while to find out which of the 56 State Boards of Nursing do not require this examination, by inquiring at the CGFNS.

1.1.2.2 Licensure Prerequisites

There are certain prerequisites for taking the CGFNS examination:

Proof of certain Years of Schooling
One prerequisite for taking this examination is the completion of a total of 12 years of consecutive schooling. If only 10 or 11 years of schooling can be shown the so called GED-test – General Education Development Test – can be taken at an accredited test center, i.e.* the Sylvan Prometric Testing Centers in Frankfurt am Main, Berlin, Munich or Hamburg. This exam tests general knowledge in such subjects as history, geography, mathematics, literature etc. As preparation for taking the test appropriate books can be purchased. Information about the test can be obtained from Sylvan Prometric (address see appendix).

Proof of Nursing Education
Proof has to be submitted that the applicant has had theoretical and clinical education in the following nursing areas: adult nursing (medical, surgical), nursing of children (maternal, infants), psychiatric/mental health nursing. This proof is submitted by way of a certificate issued by the school of nursing the applicant did her/his training at and **sent directly by the school** to the CGFNS Commission in Philadelphia.
German nurses who solely have their nursing education in pediatric or geriatric nursing are not acceptable into this system since American nursing education is based on a nursing generalist curriculum.

* id est = that is

to prepare – vorbereiten, **to contain** – beinhalten, **obtainment** – Erwerb, **to purchase** – kaufen, **majority** – Mehrheit, **to establish** – festlegen, **foreign educated** – im Ausland ausgebildet, **preparation** – Vorbereitung, **to initiate** – beginnen, **it is worth while** – es lohnt sich, **inquiring** – nachfragen, **prerequisits** – Vorleistungen, **proof** – Beleg, **completion** – Abschluss, **consecutive** – aufeinander folgend, **accredited** – anerkannt, **subjects** – Fächer, **appropriate** – einschlägig, **to submit** – vorlegen, **adult** – Erwachsener, **to issue** – herausgeben, **solely** – ausschließlich, **to accept** – annehmen

Before submitting the German nursing certificate to the CGFNS Commission it should be translated into English by a certified translator.

1.1.2.3 English Language Test

All foreign nurses have to proof that they are able to understand, speak, read and write English. For this reason all applicants have to take the *Test of English as a Foreign Language – TOEFL.* The CGFNS test and the TOEFL test should be taken within 2 years of each other. No particular sequence is required. Similar to the preparation for taking the CGFNS examination, test books and tapes are available for taking the TOEFL (i.e. Arco's TOEFL, 2000 Edition, Arco Macmillan USA, ISBN 0-02-863219-2 – see address for GED/ TOEFEL CENTER in appendix). In addition, help can be obtained from the Center for Communication in Health Care (see address in appendix).This test too can be taken at one of the Sylvan Prometric Centers (see also Buckley-Viertel 2001, page 103 ff).

1.1.2.4 Taking American State Boards

Whether the CGFNS examination has been successfully passed, or whether due to the State Board of Nursing regulation in certain states it was not taken, the nurse has to apply to the State Board of Nursing to take the National Counsel Licensure Examination = American Nursing Licensure Examination in the state in which she plans to work. Following the successful passing of this examination the nurse receives the necessary licensure to work as a nurse in the United States. With this licensure she is a registered nurse in the United States. (Commission on Graduates of Foreign Nursing Schools 2002).
Generally speaking, the nurse can not work as a nurse without a professional license.
However, certain State Boards of Nursing issue temporary licensures which will allow the nurse to work until both examinations (the CGFNS and the National Council Licensure) are completed (Commission on Graduates of Foreign Nursing Schools 2002).

Reasons for this Precaution
Having worked for many years in hospital nursing management in the United States my experience in this matter has been the following. Before the establishment of the CGFNS Commission some 25 years ago nurses came to the United States from all countries of the world.
On account of their native license they were allowed to work as an RN (registered nurse) in hospitals and other health facilities while waiting for the date on which to take the American nursing examination. A certain percentage of these nurses failed the examination. This caused problems for the nurses, as well as their superiors. Psychologically, the nurses were very disappointed and felt dejected due to their failure. In practice, they now had to work

to certify – bestätigen, **to proof** – belegen, **reason** – Ursache, **particular sequence** – bestimmte Reihenfolge, **successfully passed** – erfolgreich bestanden, **due to** – infolge von, **to apply** – beantragen, **to receive** – erhalten, **registered nurse** – in das professionnelle Register eingetragene Krankenschwester, **temporary licensure** – zeitlich begrenzte Lizenz, **to allow** – erlauben, **to complete** – abschließen, **establishment** – Errichtung, **on account of** – aufgrund von, **native** – einheimisch, **health facilities** – Gesundheitseinrichtungen, **to fail** – durchfallen, **disappointed** – enttäuscht, **dejected** – zurückgesetzt

in status and salary on the level of an untrained nursing assistant until the next time – usually several months later – they could re-take and hopefully pass the examination.
The nursing superiors felt bad having to reduce the nurses in status and salary to the lowest level in the nursing hierarchy. Responsible for the well being of their subordinates they disliked to cause them this psychological distress. But being also responsible for the safety of the patients on the basis of having officially qualified nurses attending to them they had to implement this professional regulation.
With the creation of the CGFNS Commission by the professional nursing control organizations (see State Boards of Nursing, chapter 4, Quality Patient Care) a mechanism has been set up whereby an identical level of nursing capabilities of registered nurses is assured nationwide. Needless to say that an identical level of nursing capabilities nationwide also assures a certain level of quality patient care throughout the country.
The continuous effort by national nursing organizations to maintain a certain level of nursing capabilities and thereby a certain standard of quality patient care has again been demonstrated by the statement of the National Council of State Boards of Nursing (Dachverband sämtlicher State Boards) at its meeting in October 2001: »Both domestic and international nurses need to comply with standards of approved/comparable education, hold a verified and unencumbered state license and be proficient in their written and spoken English skills. Any reduction in these standards may lead to increase in errors, risk of patient harm, and decreased public confidence« (Apple,K. 2001).

1.1.2.5 Visa

In order to be allowed to **work** and to have **unlimited stay** in the United States an H–Visa = working visa has to be obtained. Information and forms for application for a visa are available from the American consulates in major German cities. At the time of applying for a visa the certificate of the CGFNS exam – Commission on Graduates of Foreign Nursing Schools Examination – and a work contract from the prospective place of employment have to be submitted. The prospective employer has to submit a petition to the US Immigration Services in order for the immigration to be approved. In view of possible changes and individual applicant situations it is adviseable to contact the US Visa Information Service in order to get information on current regulations (Information obtained from the American Consulate Frankfurt am Main 2002, Telefon: 0190-85 00 55).

status and salary – Position und Gehalt, **to reduce** – herabsetzen, **to be responsible** – verantwortlich sein, **subordinate** – Nachgeordnete, **distress** – Stress, **safety** – Sicherheit, **to attend to** – behandeln, **professional regulations** – professionelle Vorgaben, **creation** – Errichtung, **identical level** – einheitliches Niveau, **nationwide** – landesweit, **to assure** – versichern, **effort** – Bemühen, **maintain** – erhalten, **to demonstrate** – zeigen, **domestic** – einheimisch, **to comply** – sich daran halten, **approved/comparable** – anerkannt/vergleichbar, **to verify** – beurkunden, unencumbered – unbelastet, **to be proficient** – fähig/fließend sein, **reduction** – Absenkung, **increase** – Zunahme, **decreased public confidence** – Abnahme öffentlichen Vertrauens, **application** – Antrag, **work contract** – Arbeitsvertrag, **prospective place of employment** – voraussichtlicher Arbeitsplatz, **employer** – Arbeitgeber, **petition** – Antrag, **to approve** – genehmigen, **current regulations** – aktuelle Vorgaben

Visa proceedings usuallly take several months. The possession of a working visa entitles the person to receive a »green card« = a work permit, shortly after arrival in the United States. Working on the basis of a green card a person has all the privileges Americans have with the exception of participating in political elections or sitting on a jury. A working visa, also called immigration visa does not mean the person has to immigrate to the United States, i.e. give up her/his citizenship. If desired, the person can become an American citizen after five years of entering the United States by fulfilling certain legal requirements.

1.1.2.6 A Place to Work

A good way to obtain a place to work in the United States, if not gotten with the help of friends, is to check the section of job offers in the professional journals or search in the Internet. Most job offers give the name of the nurse recruiter. **Do address** your application to this person. She is a colleague and understands your questions and requests. Write your application like you would in Germany. It is important that you:

- include all your German nursing certificates (translated),
- show proof of your continuous professional education (translated),
- stress your professional accomplishments,
- give the status of your CGFNS and TOEFL exams, (in order to save time it is possible to apply for a job while in the process of preparing for these exams),
- state the nursing specialty you want to work in,
- give the reason for your wanting to work in the USA and in that particular hospital/ facility,
- give the date of your approximate availability.

A letter of recommendation from a superior will most likely have a positive effect on the reader deciding on your employment.
During the course of your negotiations with the hospital/institution you should ask to be sent a work contract for submission to the American consulate.

1.1.2.7 Language

Since you have prepared yourself for the CGFNS exam and the TOEFL test your professional English should be quite good. Perhaps it is excellent. But keep on reading professional literature or listening to this kind of tapes regularly while you await the issuance of your visa.

possession – Besitz, **to entitle** – berechtigen, **work permit** – Arbeitserlaubnis, **privileges** – Rechte, **exception** – Ausnahme, **elections** – Wahlen, **sitting on a jury** – Schöffendienste, **to desire** – wünschen, **legal requirements** – rechtliche Vorgaben, **job offers** – Stellenangebote, **nurse recruiter** – Kr. Schwester zuständig für Anwerbung von Pflegepersonal, **colleague** – Kollegin, **requests** – Anfragen, **show proof** – belegen, **stress** – hervorheben, **accomplishments** – Fähigkeiten, **state** – angeben, **facility** – Einrichtung, **approximate availability** – ungefähre Verfügbarkeit, **letter of recommendation** – Empfehlungsschreiben, **negotiations** – Verhandlungen, **work contract** – Arbeitsvertrag, **to await** – erwarten, **issuance** – Herausgabe

2 The American Health Care System

In diesem Kapitel wird das US-amerikanische Gesundheitssystem beschrieben. Dabei werden die drei Hauptzweige der Gesundheitsversorgung skizziert. Abgeleitet davon werden zahlreiche Arten von Gesundheitsdiensten aufgezeigt und verschiedene Krankenhaustypen vorgestellt. Die zwei Säulen der öffentlichen und privaten Gesundheitsversicherung werden erläutert.

2.1 Health Care Delivery

The American health care system is one of the largest industries in the United States employing over 11 million people or approximately 10 % of the work force (O'Bryan Doheny, M. 1997). Health care is delivered to the public in many different ways.

2.1.1 The Three Major Categories of Health Care Delivery

2.1.1.1 The Public Health Agencies

These agencies are financially supported with tax funds and have a wide range of action. They coordinate and administer health programs, conduct health research, analyse health statistics and set health standards and qualifications.
One example of a public health agency is the Center of Disease Control and Prevention in Atlanta – CDC. It deals with the prevention of communicable diseases and the promotion of health. Subagencies are established at the local and state levels where they carry out their specific responsibilities, i.e. identification of environmental and individual health care needs of a certain geographic area and organizing sources to meet those needs.

2.2.1.2 The Voluntary Agencies

These are private nonprofit groups that are supported by donations and gifts, third-party payment and personal payment, as well as fee for service, fund raising, dues, publications and grants. They are not entitled to government funding. These agencies meet specific health needs in the community and may have subdivisions at the local, regional or national level. Their aim is to enhance the total health care delivery effort. Examples of such agencies are: The American Heart Association, The American Cancer Society.

public health agencies – öffentliche Gesundheitsorganisationen, **tax funds** – Steuergelder, **wide range** – großer Bereich, **to administer** – durchführen, **research** – Forschung, **communicable diseases** – ansteckende Krankheiten, **promotion** – Förderung, **state** – Bundesstaat, **responsibilities** – Aufgaben, **environment** – Umwelt, **sources** – Mittel, **voluntary** – freiwillig, **donations** – Spenden, **third party payment** – Krankenversicherungen, **fee for service** – Bezahlung für Leistung, **fund raising** – Spendensammlung, **dues** – Beiträge, **grants** – Zuwendungen, **entitled** – berechtigt, **government funding** – staatliche Gelder, **aim** – Ziel, **to enhance** – fördern, **health care delivery effort** – Gesundheitsversorgungsbemühen

2.1.1.3 The Proprietary Agencies

These are privately owned agencies. Types of such facilities are hospitals, diagnostic centers, private home health care, skilled care facilities, private practitioner's services. Some nurses, physicians, dentists, psychologists and social workers are private practitioners working on the basis of self-employment.

2.1.2 Types of Health Care Services

Individuals can enter the health care system at different levels according to their particular needs at any given time. Following, a brief description is given of the numerous types of health care services:

2.1.2.1 Prenatal Centers

In a prenatal center care is usually provided by a community health agency. Health care teaching focuses on the development of the unborn child, nutritional requirements, physical changes of the mother, birthing, child care, psychological responses to a new family member and financial plannning.
The location of such a center can be in certain rooms of a school, a church or a hospital.

2.1.2.2 Birthing Centers

A birthing center creates a home like setting where family members can be present during delivery of a child. Professional staff in the person of a midwife is present.
A birthing center may adjoin a hospital or be an independent community facility.

2.1.2.3 Well Child Centers

Well child centers assist the family in the care of their growing child. Centers may be located in clinics, schools or churches. These centers provide for health assessment (i.e. physical examination, developmental screening procedures), illness prevention (i.e. immunizations, parenting education, home safety practices) and nutritional counseling.

proprietary – in Privatbesitz, **skilled care facilities** – Einrichtungen mit professionellem Pflegedienst, **private practitioners** – privat Praktizierende, **self** – employment – Selbstständigkeit, **health care services** – Gesundheitsdienste, **nutritional requirements** – Ernährungsbedürfnisse, **birthing** – Entbindung, **responses** – Reaktionen, **delivery** – Entbindung, **staff** – Mitarbeiter, **midwife** – Hebamme, **present** – anwesend, **to adjoin** – anschließen, **independent** – selbstständig, **well child** – gesundes Kind, **to provide** – verfügbar machen, **development** – Entwicklung

2.1.2.4 Educational Systems

Elementary and secondary educational systems teach courses in health care. The aim is to educate children and adolescents in health maintenance and self-care. A special focus is on healthy life styles, human sexuality and drug abuse. Screening programs are conducted within schools for early detection of visual, hearing and dental problems, as well as, obesity and scoliosis. Certain immunization programs are carried out.

2.1.2.5 Health Maintenance Organizations – HMOs

The health maintenance organizations are designed to prevent illness and decrease the need for hospitalization or the length of hospitalization. They provide comprehensive health care services for the whole family at certain rates of prepaid fees (see section Health Insurance). There are four types of HMOs:

1. *Staff.* Health care services are provided by an established group practice, health professionals are employed directly by the HMO.
2. *Group.* The HMO contracts with a group practice to provide health care. The group is paid on a capitation basis.
3. *Network.* Two or more group practices with various specialties are contracted to provide health care.
4. *Individualized Practice Association.* Individual professionals are contracted to provide health care to HMO-clients as well as their own patients.

2.1.2.6 Industry

Industry, in an effort to promote health has set up screening programs for employees for hearing, visual and other health related problems (i.e. alcoholism, diabetes, hypertension).Due to industrial and governmental control, such as the federal Occupational Safety and Health Act (OSHA) safety measures have been instituted in the areas of noise abatement and environmental hazard control. Other primary health services offered are health education, counseling and referral services for identified problems.

2.1.2.7 Ambulatory Care Centers

Nurse managed centers are community-based, nurse-run clinics. Types of services include birthing centers, wellness programs, long term continuity care, support services for care givers of patients with debilitating diseases such as Alzheimer's.

elementary and secondary educational systems – Grundschule und höhere Bildungssysteme, **adolescents** – Jugendliche, **maintenance** – Erhaltung, **abuse** – Missbrauch, **to prevent** – verhindern, **to decrease** – absenken, **comprehensive health care** – umfassende Gesundheitsversorgung, **prepaid fees** – im voraus gezahlte Beiträge, **employed** – angestellt, **to contract** – vertraglich festlegen, **group practice** – Gruppenpraxis, **capitation** – Deckelung der Kostenerstattung, **various** – vielseitig, **to promote** – fördern, **safety measures** – Sicherheitsmaßnahmen, **noise abatement** – Lärmbeseitigung, **environmental hazard** – Umweltgefahr, **referral services** – Überweisungsdienste, **nurse-run** – von Krankenschwestern geführt, **birthing centers** – Entbindungszentren, **support services** – Unterstützungsdienste, **debilitating** – invalidisierend

2.1.2.8 Clinics

Clinics provide early diagnosis and treatment. They may be affiliated with a hospital but can be run independently. Clients enter a clinic, obtain treatment and return home. Clinics typically deal with: eye disorders, medical clinics with internal disorders such as gastro-intestinal ulcers and heart disease, surgical clinics perform minor surgery or follow up after surgery in hospital, orthopedic clinics take care of clients with fractures and post joint replacements, dermatology clinics treat patients with skin disorders and weight control clinics take care of obese clients.

2.1.2.9 Physicians Offices and Private Practice

Health care services in physicians' offices concentrate on diagnosis, treatment and follow-up care for specific illness. This care is usually given on an ambulatory basis. Entry for most people into the health care delivery system is through the physician. Many physicians practice medicine in their established offices and have admitting and treatment privileges at nearby hospitals.

2.1.2.10 Community Mental Health Centers

The focus of care for these clients is in a community setting rather than in a hospital. Therefore these centers function on an outpatient basis. Clients come for diagnosis and treatment of emotional dysfunctions or dysfunctions related to crisis. It is the goal of the clinic setting to help clients function within society while participating in treatment close to their home and families.

2.1.2.11 Services for Rehabilitation

These services aim to attain the maximum ability of function for and with the client and to help him realize his strengths and limitations. Clients enter rehabilitation facilities by referrals from health care providers.

2.1.2.12 Specialized Rehabilitation Hospitals

Rehabilitation hospitals provide extended care for clients who no longer require the acute care services of a hospital but need further care and training to cope with their illness or change in functioning. Specialized personnel and equipment are available to deal with long term problems. Typical clients in this facility may be persons with a cerebral vascular accident = CVA (in lay term: stroke), or spinal cord injury with paralysis.

treatment – Behandlung, **affiliated** – angeschlossen, **surgery** – Chirurgie, **follow up** – Nachsorge, **joint replacement** – Gelenkersatz, **disorders** – Erkrankungen, **physician** – Arzt, **health care delivery system** – Gesundheitsversorgungssystem, **admitting and treatment privileges** – Aufnahme- und Behandlungserlaubnis, **dysfunction** – Bewältigungsunfähigkeit, **goal** – Ziel, **to realize** – wahrnehmen, **referrals** – Überweisungen, **health care providers** – Leistungserbringer, **extended** – verlängert, **to cope** – bewältigen, **equipment** – Geräte, **long term** – langzeitlich, **cerebral vascular accident** – Apoplexie, **lay term** – Laiensprache, **injury** – Verletzung

2.1.2.13 Skilled Nursing Facilities

Skilled nursing facilities are for clients no longer needing acute care in hospitals, but still needing continued professional nursing care. This kind of care is provided with the aim that they may reach their optimal level of functioning within the facility or in their homes.

2.1.2.14 Hospices

Hospices provide services for the terminally ill persons and their families. The goal of the hospice movement is to maintain persons in their home environment and create together with them their individual level of quality of life. Emotional support and physical assistance (i.e. pain control) are given in the person's home, as well as in the hospice facility.

2.1.2.15 Community Health Agencies

Community health agencies meet the health needs of individuals, families, groups and communities. They include public health agencies, home nursing services, visiting nurse associations and nursing clinics and centers. Community agencies may function as clinics for ambulatory clients or be structured so that the health care provider sees the client within the home setting. Since the community agencies are concerned about the health needs of a diverse clientele, the skills of various health personnel are required in order to determine the extent of need for prevention, detection, diagnosis and rehabilitation (see O'Bryan Doheny, M. et al 1997).

2.1.3 Types of Hospitals

The American Hospital Association classifies hospitals in several ways. There are short and long term hospitals, as well as specialty hospitals (i.e. orthopedic, cancer), teaching, non-teaching and independent hospitals, or those that are part of a multihospital system, public and private hospitals, non-profit and for-profit (investor-owned) hospitals. Following, four types of hospitals are described.

2.1.3.1 Teaching Hospitals

There are nonfederal hospitals belonging to the Council of Teaching Hospitals and Health Systems (COTH) of the Association of American Medical Colleges. These COTH hospitals represent 6 % of all hospitals. Relative to the other hospitals, COTH hospitals are larger and usually located in large urban areas. Because of their commitment to education, research and patient care COTH hospitals deliver a large percentage of tertiary or highly complex services.

skilled nursing facilities – Einrichtungen mit professionellem Pflegedienst, **hospice movement** – Hospizbewegung, **community** – Gemeinde, **health agency** – Gesundheitsorganisation, **public** – öffentlich, **visiting nurse association** – häusliche Pflege, **provider** – Leistungserbringer, **concerned** – befasst, **diverse clientele** – unterschiedliches Klientel, **health personnel** – Gesundheitspersonal, **required** – erforderlich, **extent** – Ausmaß, **detection** – Aufdeckung, **nonfederal** – nichtstaatlich, **relative** – im Vergleich, **urban** – städtisch, **commitment** – Verpflichtung, **to deliver** – durchführen

2.1.3.2 Multihospital Systems

In recent years multihospital systems have proliferated. This means that one or more hospitals are under the contracted management of another hospital, or are legally incorporated in a larger structure of several hospitals under one general administration. This way hospitals are becoming parts of larger health systems in that such systems usually provide diversified services, such as surgery, ambulatory care, rehabilitation, home health services, skilled nursing, psychiatric care, and alcohol/drug dependency facilities and services.

2.1.3.3 Rural Hospitals

Rural hospitals are located away from large cities in the country. They draw their clientele from persons working in farming, mining, energy and oil production, large federal, state or local government installations. Rural hospitals are usually small with a bed capacity of approximately 100 beds or less. Increasingly, rural hospitals join together to more efficiently purchase and utilize equipment and materials.

2.1.3.4 Public Hospitals

Public hospitals are owned by agencies of federal, state and local governments. Federal hospitals have been established to serve special groups: American Indians, merchant seamen, military personnel and veterans. There are also state university or teaching hospitals that provide short-term general acute care.

There are two different types of short-term general public hospitals by ownership.

The first type has characteristics similar to the smaller nonprofit hospital, is located in small towns, is used by private attending physicians and serves paying and indigent patients. Both types may be owned by a city or county government department.

The second type is located in major urban areas. The physicians are mostly salaried and work either for the hospital directly or for medical school clinical practice plans. The larger public hospitals rely heavily on medical residents in training to provide physician services.

Increasingly, like those in the private sector public hospitals are seeking alternative structures, like forming nonprofit corporations or entering into public-private mergers or partnerships (see Jonas, Kovner 1999).

to proliferate – ausbreiten, **contracted** – vertraglich geregelt, **legally incorporated** – rechtlich eingeordnet, **administration** – Betriebsleitung, **diversified** – vielfältig, **skilled nursing** – professionelle Pflege, **dependency** – Abhängigkeit, **rural** – ländlich, **mining** – Bergbau, **installations** – Einrichtungen, **to utilize** – einsetzen, **public** – öffentlich, **federal** – bundesstaatlich, **governments** – Behörden, **merchant seamen** – Handelsmarine, **short-term** – kurzeitig, **private attending physicians** – privat behandelnde Ärzte, **indigent** – mittellos, **county** – Landkreis, **salaried** – angestellt, **medical school clinical practice plans** – klinische Praxispläne in der medizinischen Ausbildung, **rely** – sich verlassen, **medical residents in training** – Ärzte in Ausbildung, **physician services** – ärztliche Versorgung, **to seek** – suchen, **merger** – Zusammenschluss

2.1.4 Health Care Insurance

Health care insurance in the United States has been undergoing continuous change during the past 30 years and is still in flux. This means that certain systems in use today may well be obsolete in the near future and new ones may be created. Following are some of the currently most common health insurance systems. These are devided in the public and the private insurance sector.

2.1.4.1 The Public Insurance Sector

Medicare

Medicare was legally enacted in 1965. It ensures 39 million persons against the financial consequences of acute illness. This plan consists of two parts: Part A covers hospital services, Part B covers physician services. Some 151 million employees make mandatory contributions to Medicare's Part A Hospital Insurance Trust Fund during their working years in oder to receive benefits when they retire. This means, this health insurance benefits persons over the age of 65. All eligible beneficiaries are automatically enrolled in Part A, which finances inpatient hospital services, continued treatment or rehabilitation in a skilled nursing facility, and hospice care.

Medicare's Part B is voluntary, although a great majority of beneficiaries participate in this insurance. Part B pays for physicians' services and outpatient hospital services, including emergency room visits, ambulatory surgery, diagnostic tests, laboratory services and durable medical equipment. Under Part B medicare pays 80 percent of the approved amount (according to a fee schedule) for covered services in excess of an annual deductable of $ 100. The funding of this part comes primarily from people who are less than 65 years old, through payroll taxes, income taxes and interest on the trust fund. 11 percent comes from the monthly premiums payed by elderly beneficiaries (see Iglehart, John 1999).

Medicaid

Medicaid is the largest health insurer in the United States in terms of eligible beneficiaries, covering medical services and long term care for 41.3 million persons. In 1997 Medicaid spent $ 159.9 billion (12.4 percent of total national health care expenditures) for covered services for low income people who were elderly, blind, disabled, receiving public assistance, or among the working poor.

health care insurance – Krankenversicherung, **currently** – derzeit, **legally enacted** – rechtlich festgelegt, **mandatory contributions** – Pflichtbeiträge, **benefits** – Nutzen, **to retire** – in Rente gehen, **eligible beneficiaries** – berechtigte Nutzer, **treatment** – Behandlung, **voluntary** – freiwillig, **durable medical equipment** – haltbare medizinische Geräte, **approved amount** – bewilligte Summe, **fee schedule** – Bewilligungsraster, **covered services** – abgedeckte Behandlungen, **annual deductable** – jährliche Selbstbeteiligung, **in excess** – darüberliegend, **funding** – Finanzierung, **payroll taxes** – Einkommensteuer, **interest on the trust fund** – Zinsertrag aus der Anlage, **monthly premiums** – monatliche Beiträge, **to cover** – abdecken, **long term** – über längere Zeit, **disabled** – behindert, **to receive** – erhalten

Medicaid is the main public insurance program for many people of limited income. Over the past decade the national expansion in Medicaid's eligible population was driven by federal requirements to increase health care insurance coverage for pregnant women and for children, people of low income and disabled persons. Medicaid is largely administered by the individual States. Medicaid beneficiaries account for about 11 percent of a State's population, but some States have considerably higher percentages.
Being poor does not automatically make a person eligible for Medicaid. In fact, in 1997 Medicaid covered only 44.4 percent of nonelderly persons with an annual income of less than $ 13,300 for a family of three. Most people become eligible by meeting a federally defined criterion (i.e. advanced age, blindness, disability, membership in a single-parent family with dependent children). Within the federal guidelines the states set their own criteria for eligibility with respect to income and assets, resulting in large variations in coverage from State to State (see Iglehart, John 1999).

2.1.4.2 The Private Insurance Sector

Health Maintenance Organizations – HMOs
HMOs are financed by the client or his employer paying a monthly premium and a small charge for each visit to the clinic. The typical HMO provides a wide range of services such as preventive services and educational materials, as well as comprehensive health care. Many HMOs are big medical clinics with doctors, nurses and different specialized therapists on staff. The client has to choose a doctor from the organizations own list. This doctor will coordinate the patient's medical treatment. Comprehensive treatment and care is delivered within the system of managed care. HMOs tend to provide the least expensive medical treatment by taking care of patients as much as possible on an out patient basis (http://moneycentral.msn/quickref/quickref.asp?Cat=10&SelCat=2&RefType=0& 12/2001).

Preferred Provider Organization – PPO
PPOs and HMOs are very similar. Both types of insurance plans offer broad health care coverage and their insurance premiums are relatively low. The cost of each clinic visit is nominal. The main difference between the two insurance plans is the choice of physician by the client.
In the HMO plan the client has to choose a physician from the list of doctors the organization has chosen. In the PPO plan the client can continue to be taken care of by his family doctor or any other doctor he desires. However, if the client chooses a doctor or hospital which is not on the list of preferred providers, the insurance generally pays only half of the total cost (Lit. see above-internet).
Employees of hospitals have health insurance provided for them by the hospital. This is considered one of the employment benefits (see chapter 6, section 4 benefits).

public insurance – staatliche Versicherung, **expansion** – Erweiterung, **requirements** – Anforderungen, **coverage** – Abdeckung, **pregnant women** – schwangere Frauen, **to administer** – verwalten, **federal guidelines** – staatliche Richtlinien, **assets** – Besitz, **variations in coverage** – Unterschiede in der Abdeckung, **employer** – Arbeitgeber, **charge** – Gebühr, **therapists on staff** – angestellte Therapeuten, **least expensive** – preiswerteste, **preferred provider** – bevorzugter Leistungserbringer, **insurance** – Versicherung, **nominal** – minimal, **benefit** – Zusatzleistung

Blue Cross and Blue Shield
This insurance agency offers two main types of health insurance. One type is for persons under the age of 65, which is the retirement age. The other is for persons over 65 years of age.

Insurance under 65 years of age

Coverage
The insurance under 65 years of age covers the following health services:
Physician Office Services,
Hospital/Inpatient Care,
Outpatient/Clinic Treatment,
Ambulatory Surgery Treatment,
Emergency Services,
Mental Health Services,
Medications,
Special Services:
  Hospice Care,
  Skilled Nursing Facility – 90 days per Calendar Year,
  Home Health Care,
  Ambulance,
  Durable Medical Equipment,
  Prosthetics and Orthotics.

Payments
The insured pays monthly premiums. There is a choice of an annual deductible of $ 500, $ 1000 or $ 2000. Overall insurance costs can be reduced if the insured choses to opt for a family physician of a PPO-Group – Preferred Provider Organization (see above).
For every service listed above a certain amount of copayment has to be made except for the Special Services. It is interesting to note that the copayment for medications is least when the insured uses generic drugs. It increases when preferred brand name drugs are taken and is highest for non-preferred drugs (BlueCross BlueShield, 2003).

retirement – Ruhestand, **coverage** – Abdeckung, **physician's office** – Arztpraxis, **medications** – Arzneimittel, **home health** – Häusliche Pflege, **prosthetics** – Prothesen, **orthotics** – Stützhilfen/Korsette, **deductible** – Selbstbeteiligung, **overall** – gesamt, **the insured** – der Versicherte, **to chose** – auswählen, **to opt** – entscheiden, **copayment** – Selbstbeteiligung, **is least** – ist am geringsten, **preferred brand name** – bekannter Markenname, **drug** – Arzneimittel

Insurance over 65 years of age

Coverage
The second type of insurance is for persons over 65 years of age. This insurance is in addition to Medicare (see above) and is called the Medicare Supplement Insurance. This means that this type of insurance covers certain costs which are only partially covered by Medicare. There are four different plans, each with a different extent of coverage, to chose from. These supplementary plans cover mainly expenses for:

- Hospital Care,
- Outpatient Services,
- Physician Services,
- At-Home-Recovery Care,
- Medical Care necessary in a foreign country

Payments
The monthly premium payments are based on the age of the person at the time of enrollment.
Each of the four insurance plans require different monthly premiums. Similar to the system of copayment for insured persons under the age of 65, here too most services entail a certain amount of copayment (BlueShield BlueCross, 2003).

non-preferred – unbekannter Markenname, **in addition** – zusätzlich, **partially covered** – teilweise abgedeckt, **supplement** – Ergänzung, **expenses** – Kosten, **recovery** – Wiederherstellung, **foreign country** – Ausland, **payment** – Zahlung, **premium** – Beitrag, **enrollment** – Beitritt, **to require** – erfordern, **to entail** – nach sich ziehen

3 The Hospital

In diesem Kapitel wird anhand eines Organigramms beispielhaft die Organisationsstruktur eines Krankenhauses aufgezeigt und das betriebliche Selbstverständnis und das damit einhergehende betriebliche Leitbild vorgestellt. Es werden die Kategorien von angestellten und nicht angestellten Ärzten skizziert und dabei auf die Bedeutung letzterer für den Betrieb hingewiesen. Die Stellung von Patienten sowie deren Rechte und Pflichten werden veranschaulicht. Weiterhin wird auf die Grundlagen und Funktionsweise einer Ethik-Kommission eingegangen. Abschließend werden Wesen und Kontrollmechanismen einer außerbetrieblichen Qualitätssicherungs-Kommission erläutert.

3.1 Organization

American hospitals have a written organization plan. This plan **delineates** the way information is distributed and **responsibility is shouldered**. The overall responsibility for the hospital is with the Board of Directors. The day to day operations, meaning the daily functioning of the hospital is the **sole** responsibility of the Executive Director. There is no **tripartite** form of hospital administration. Consequently, the Medical Staff and the Director of Nursing are not on the same level with the Executive Director.Generally speaking, the organization plan of American hospitals is similar to the one shown in Figure 1.

The Organization Chart of Cedar's Medical Center in Miami, Florida represents the organization of a 500 bed private hospital. Looking at it from the top down you see the *Board of Directors*. On the same level is the *Medical Staff* (see chapter 3, physicians). Following the line down you see on the left *Internal Audit*. The next step down is the *Executive Director*. This person can also be called the Chief Executive Officer, commonly abbreviated, the CEO. On the same level with him are the *Auxiliary*.

In the next line far over to the left you find *Development and Community Relations*. Connected with this department are the **Volunteers**. Next is the Department of *Marketing und Public Relations* with **Medical Media** and *International Relations*.

to delineate – skizzieren, **to shoulder responsibility** – Verantwortung tragen, **sole** – einzig, **tripartite** – dreiteilig, **Board of Directors** – Verwaltungsrat, **Medical Staff** – Ärzteschaft, **Internal Audit** – betriebsinterne Kontrollstelle, **Executive Director** – Betriebsleiter, **Auxiliary** – ehrenamtliche Hilfsdienste, **Development and Community Relations** – Entwicklung und Gemeindearbeit, **Volunteers** – ehrenamtliche Helfer/innen, **Marketing and Public Relations** – Vermarktung und Öffentlichkeitsarbeit, **Medical Media** – medizinische Medien z. B. Fotolabor, **International Relations** – internationale Beziehungen bezogen auf Patienten, **chart** – Plan

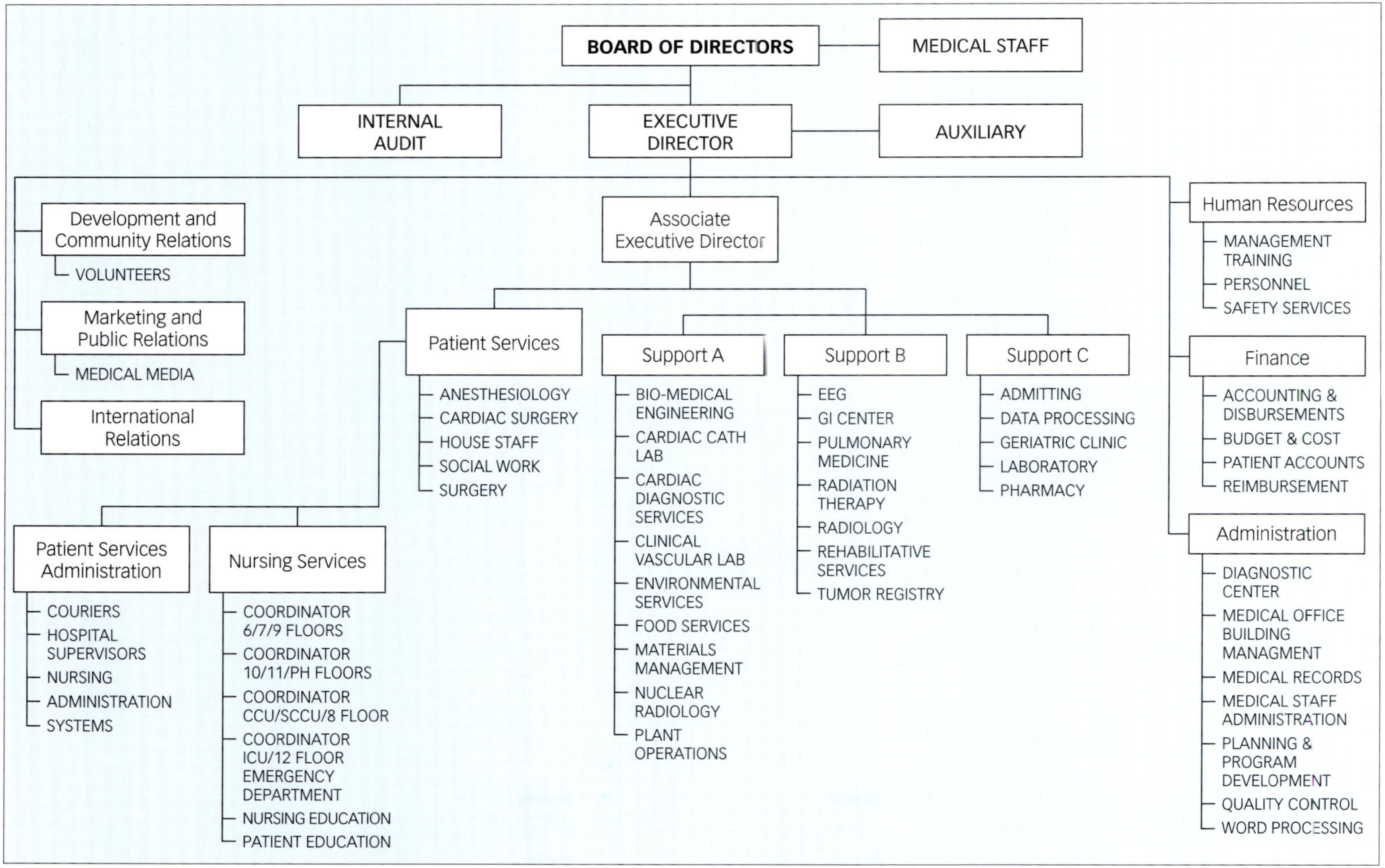

Fig. 1: Cedar's organisation chart, Cedars Medical Center, Miami, Florida.

Looking along the horizontal line to the far right, you see *Human Resources* with Management Training, Personnel and Safety Services.
The next department is *Finances* with Accounting and Disbursements, Budget and Cost, Patient Accounts and Reimbursement.

The next department is *Administration* of the Diagnostic Center, Medical Office Building, Medical Records, Medical Staff Administration, Planning & Program Development, Quality Control, Word Processing.

Going back to the central line of the chart you see the position of the *Associate Executive Director*.
Following the line to the left you find *Patient Services* consisting of three columns. The first column on the left shows the department of *Patient Services Administration* with Couriers, Hospital Supervisors, Nursing Administration, Systems.
The second column to the right shows *Nursing Services*. You can see how the different floors and intensive care units are divided. Each group of floors and intensive care units have a Coordinator. In this department is also Nursing Education and Patient Education located.

The third column to the right shows ***Anesthesiology, Cardiac Surgery***, *House Staff*, ***Social Work***, *Surgery*.

Next you see on the right a complex of three columns. These are so called *Support Departments*:

Support Department A consists of the following specialties:
Bio-Medical Engineering – Biomedizinische Technik,
Cardiac Cath Lab = Cardiac Catheterization Laboratory,
Cardiac Diagnostic Services,

Human Resources – Personalabteilung, **Management Training** – Managementausbildung, **Personnel** – Mitarbeiter, **Safety Services** – Sicherheitsdienst, **Finances** – Finanzen, **Accounting and Disbursement** – Buchhaltung und Ausgaben, **Budget and Cost** – Budget und Kosten, **Patient Accounts** – Patienten Konten, **Reimbursement** – Kostenerstattung, **Administration** – Administration/Management des Diagnosezentrums, **Medical Office Building** – Gebäude mit Arztpraxen, Gesundheitsdiensten, **Medical Records** – Archiv für Krankenakten, **Medical Staff Administration** – Mangement/Betreuung der Belegärzte, **Planning and Programm Development** – Planung und Entwicklung von Service-Programmen, **Word-Processing** – Computer Abteilung, **Associate Executive Director** – stellvertretender Betriebsleiter, **Patient Services** – Patientenversorgung, **Patient Services Administration** – Patientenversorgung Management, **Couriers** – Hol- und Bringedienst, **Hospital Supervisors** – Abteilungsleiter/innen, **Nursing Administration** – Abteilung Pflegedienst, **Systems** – betriebsinterne Systeme, **Nursing Services** – Pflegedienst, **floors** – Pflegestationen, **to divide** – aufteilen, **Coordinators** – pflegerische Abteilungsleitungen, **Nursing Education** – innerbetriebliche Fortbildung, **Patient Education** – Patientengesundheitserziehung, **House Staff** – angestellte Ärzte, **Surgery** – Operationsabteilung, **Support Departments** – unterstützende Abteilungen

Cardio Vascular Lab = Cardio Vascular Laboratory – Gefäßlabor,
Environmental Services – Umwelt Management/Reinigungsdienste,
Food Service – Speisenversorgung,
Materials Management – Materialabteilung/Einkauf,
Nuclear Radiology,
Plant Operations – Technische Abteilung.

Support Department B consists of the following specialties:
EEG
GI Center = Gastro-Intestinal Center – Endoskopie,
Pulmonary Medicine,
Radiation Therapy – Strahlentherapie,
Radiology = X-Ray Department – Röntgenabteilung,
Rehabilitative Services,
Tumor Registry

Support Department C consists of the following specialties:
Admitting – Patientenaufnahme,
Data Processing – Datenverarbeitung,
Geriatric Clinic,
Laboratory – Klinisches Labor,
Pharmacy – Apotheke

All hospital departments work 8-hour shifts on 7 days a week. This means a typical work day is divided into three shifts. The morning shift begins at 7.00 a.m. The afternoon shift at 3 p.m. and the night shift at 11 p.m. The clinical departments, i.e. the laboratory, EKG, radiology, pharmacy are fully staffed on the first two shifts from 7 a.m.–11 p.m., on 7 days a week. On the night shift = 11 p.m.–7 a.m. these departments run on minimal staffing. The admission department is staffed 24 hours on 7 days a week.

3.2 Mission Statement

At the founding of a hospital the purpose or the mission of the hospital is declared in written form. The reason for this is the idea that *»each institution exists for a specific purpose or mission and to fulfill a specific social function. For health care institutions this means health care services to maintain health, cure illness and allay pain and suffering«* (*Rowland and Rowland*, 1992: 127). The mission statement is revised as changes in services occur.
A mission statement may read as follows: *»St. John's Hospital provides to the people of Central Illinois a ministry of value-based services in the Catholic tradition of compassionate care, justice, and reverence for life throughout its continuum«* (Mission Statement St. John's Hospital Springfield, Illinous 2001, Employee Handbook).

staffed – mit Personal besetzt, **founding** – Errichtung, **purpose** – Zweck, **mission statement** – Aussage zur Aufgabe, **to declare** – festlegen, **allay** – lindern, **to revise** – überarbeiten, **to occur** – auftreten, **ministry** – Dienstleistung, **value-based** – auf ideellen Werten basierend, **compassionate care** – einfühlsame Betreuung, **justice** – Gerechtigkeit, **reverence for life** – Achtung vor dem Leben

This mission statement is made known to all employees in that it is printed on the first page of the Employee's Handbook, which every employee receives at the time of employment. The meaning of it is discussed with new employees during their orientation period (see chapter 6, nursing orientation).

3.3 Philosophy

Accompanying the mission statement is the philosophy of the hospital. These two go together. The written philosophy »*explains the beliefs that determine how the mission or purpose is achieved. It gives direction to achieving purpose … It sets the character and tone of service*« (*Rowland and Rowland* 1992: 127).
Following here are some excerpts taken from the philosophy of St. John's Hopital in Springfield, Illinois. St. John's Hospital is in the ownership of a religious order. It belongs to the Sisters of the Third Order of St. Francis:

WE BELIEVE every person is created in the image of God, and therefore, has an intrinsic dignity and value. Every human life is a gift from God which must be respected, preserved with care and supported from the moment of conception until death.

WE BELIEVE those who join together to render care are part of a community. Leaders strive to create a caring climate which emphasizes hospitality and reflects the Gospel values of love, justice, service and compassion. These qualities shape the relationships between those who are serving and those who are served. Given a participation in decisions which affect them as individuals they come to know that they are accepted, understood and loved.

WE BELIEVE quality patient care requires a level of excellence which reflects the biblical vision of health as wholeness, and is, therefore, directed to the whole person – body, mind and spirit.

to make known – bekannt machen, **employer** – Angestellter, **time of employment** – zur Zeit der Anstellung, **meaning** – Bedeutung, **orientation period** – Einführungszeit, **to accompany** – begleiten, **philosophy** – Leitbild, **beliefs** – Einstellungen/Auffassungen, **to determine** – bestimmen, **to achieve** – erreichen, **character** – Wesen, **excerpts** – Auszüge, **ownership** – Besitz, **intrinsic dignity** – inhärente Würde, **to preserve** – bewahren, **to support** – unterstützen, **conception** – Empfängnis, **to render care** – pflegen, **to strive** – sich bemühen, **caring climate** – fürsorgliche Atmosphäre, **to emphasize** – betonen, **hospitality** – Gastfreundschaft, **Gospel** – Evangelium, **compassion** – Mitleid/Empathie, **to shape** – bestimmen, **relationship** – Beziehung, **those who are serving** – diejenigen, die dienen/Leistungserbringer, **those who are served** – diejenigen die bedient werden/Leistungsempfänger, **decisions which affect them** – Entscheidungen, die sie betreffen, **accepted** – anerkannt, **to reflect** – widerspiegeln, **health as wholeness** – Gesundheit als Ganzheit, **directed to** – ausgerichtet auf

WE BELIEVE educational programs for patients, families, medical staff, employees and the community-at-large promote personal and professional growth and keep alive the ideals of »healing like Jesus did« (Excerpted from the Employee Handbook, St. John's Hospital, Springfield, Illinois, 2001).

Like the mission statement the philosophy of the hospital is printed in the employee handbook. And like the mission statement the philosophy is discussed with new employees. All employees are expected to incorporate the ideas of both into the way they approach and interact with patients.

3.4 Physicians

In chapter 2 the different types of hospitals existing in the United States were explained. In these different hospitals there are those physicians who are employed by the hospital and others who work there but are not employed.

3.4.1 Physicians employed by the Hospital

In the publicly financed hospitals the majority of physicians is employed by the hospital. The private hospitals employ some physicans in specialty areas like the laboratory, the cardiac catheterization laboratory, critical care units, emergency departments and others. In addition to these medical specialists they employ a so called medical house staff. These are usually called residents. Their duties consist of giving medical care to patients throughout the hospital whenever needed and especially in emergency situations.

3.4.2 Physicians not employed by the Hospital

In private hospitals the majority of physicians is not employed by the hospital. These physicians have their private practice in town or in a medical office building near the hospital, where they treat their private patients. They have admitting privileges at one or more private hospitals. When necessary, they admit their patients to a private hospital and they treat these patients throughout their stay at the hospital. (Diese Art der medizinischen Versorgung ist dem deutschen Belegarztsystem ähnlich.)

These private physicians are the foundation for the existence of the private hospitals. As long as they are satisfied with the services the hospital provides and the way the services are provided they will send their patients. As long as patients feel well taken care of by the hospital staff they will report back positively to their doctor who in turn will send more patients.

medical staff – ärztliches Personal, **community at large** – Allgemeinheit, **are expected** – wird von ihnen erwartet, **to incorporate** – integrieren, **the way** – die Art und Weise, **to approach** – herantreten, **publicly finanzed** – staatlich finanziert, **medical house staff** – angestellte Ärzte, **duties** – Aufgaben, **to treat** – behandeln, **admitting privileges** – Aufnahme-Erlaubnis, **to admit** – aufnehmen, **stay** – Verweildauer, **foundation** – Grundlage, **well taken care of** – gut betreut, **staff** – Personal, **in turn** – wiederum

Therefore it is very important for the survival of the private hospital that the administration and the employees stay on good terms with the private physicians.
A medium seize hospital (i.e. 500 beds) may have dozens of physicians in the different medical specialties. Each specialty group elects from among their group a chief physician for a certain time period. This chief physician is entitled to advise, check and correct his colleagues in his group on medical matters. This is done in a collegial manner since the chief physician is not in a superior position to his colleagues.

3.5 Patients

In the American Hospitals the patient is the focus of attention. This can be understood by taking a look at the information booklet every patient receives at the time of admission. Following, excerpts from the Patient Information Booklet of Cedars Medical Center in Miami, Florida, are introduced.

3.5.1 The Patient Information Booklet

The Patient Information Booklet contains information about different aspects of the patient's hospital stay. First, the patient is addressed by a welcome note and an introduction to the hospital.

Under the aspect of **Admission** the patient is informed about the importance of consent forms. Explanations are given how medications he brought with him from home are being handled. Advice is given as to the protection of his valuables.

Since **every Patient** receives an identification bracelet the reason for this action is explained as follows: »*Upon admission, you will be given an identification bracelet. All of your tests and procedures will be identified by the number on your bracelet. Please, leave it on at all times and do not remove it until you leave the hospital.*« This safety measure has been in practice in hospitals for decades and is part of quality assurance (see Fig. 2).

Under the aspect of **Your Room** information is given to electrical appliances, the nurse-call, television, telephone and smoking. The possible use of bed rails is explained.

Under the aspect of **Your Hospital Stay** tests and examinations, medications, anesthesia, surgery and meals are addressed.

survival – Überleben, **stay on good terms** – gute Beziehungen unterhalten, **to elect** – wählen, **entitled** – befugt, **focus of attention** – Fokus des Geschehens, **admission** – Aufnahme, **to introduce** – vorstellen, **hospital stay** – Krankenhausaufenthalt, **to address** – ansprechen, **welcome note** – Willkommensgruß, **introduction** – Einführung, **consent forms** – Formulare zur Einwilligungserklärung, **valuables** – Wertsachen, **identification bracelet** – Identifikations-Armband, **action** – Maßnahme, **procedures** – Untersuchungen, **in practice** – wird durchgeführt, **electrical appliances** – elektrische Geräte, **nurse call** – Rufanlage, **bed rails** – Bettgitter, **examinations** – Untersuchungen, **surgery** – Operationen

3

Admission

You're here! Now what? First thing, of course, you'll be asked for some information. Each patient, or legal guardian, will be asked to sign forms authorizing the hospital and physicians to provide treatment and/ or surgery. Consents for minors must be signed by parents or guardians.

Consent forms

Even though you sign consent forms when admitted, others may be necessary for specific procedures.

Identification bracelets

Upon admission, you will be given an identification bracelet. All of your tests and procedures will be identified by the number on your bracelet. Please leave it on at all times and don't remove it until you leave the hospital.

Medications from home

If any medicines are required during your stay, your doctor will prescribe them. In the event that you brought any medication of your own, please send it home with a friend or relative. If that is not possible, give it to a nurse, who will send it to the pharmacy. Remember to ask your nurse to return your medication prior to discharge.

Valuables

We strongly advise you to leave valuables, such as jewelry, money and credit cards, at home. Otherwise, upon admission you will be asked to send such items home. If necessary you can deposit items in a "valuables envelope," which will be stored in the hospital safe. The hospital cannot be responsible for money and other valuables kept in your room. Unnecessary clothing should also be sent home.

Please keep dentures and eyeglasses in protective containers when not in use. The hospital cannot be responsible for their loss or damage.

You may pick up valuables from the Cashier's Office weekdays between 8 a.m. and 5 p.m. only. On weekends you may pick up valuables from the Admitting Office between 7 a.m. and 11 p.m. only.

Fig. 2: THE PATIENT Information Booklet, Cedars Medical Center, Miami, Florida.

Under the aspect of **Special People** the work of auxilians and volunteers, patient education, clinical nurse specialists, (see Chapter 4, Nursing Personnel) private duty nurses, (see Chapter 5, Nursing Personnel) consumer relations and case management are explained.

Under the aspect of **Special Services** beauticians and barber services, bingo-in-bed, chapel, clergy, international center, interpreters, mail, newspaper, notary public, patient library, special occasions and special services for the handicapped are described.

Under the aspect of **For You and Your Visitors** the cafeteria and the restaurant are introduced. How to order a guest tray and hotel accommodations are explained. Visiting hours for critical care, hospital security and parking is described. Attention is called to the gift shop.

Under the aspect of **Financial Information** financial counseling is offered to patients with private insurance or medicare (see chapter 2, Health Care Insurance), without insurance, and to those who want to discuss their medical bill.

Under the aspect of **Going Home** the planning and methods for the discharge of the patient are described.

Under the aspect of Advance Directives the patient's right to accept or refuse medical treatment for the purpose to prolong his life artificially is explained. He is assured of assistance should he decide to write a »Living Will«, whereby the patient declares his wishes in case of his inability of making decisions about his life or death (see Chapter 6, Emergencies).

The largest part of the booklet is designated to **Patients' Rights and** Responsibilities. Excerpts from this part read as follows:

patient education – patientenbezogene Gesundheitserziehung, **consumer relations** – hausinterne Patientenanlaufstelle, **beauticians and barber services** – Schönheits- und Friseurdienste, **clergy** – Geistliche, **notary public** – Notar, **patient library** – Patientenbibliothek, **special occasions** – besondere Anlässe, **handicapped** – Behinderte, **guest tray** – Besucheressen im Krankenzimmer, **hotel accommodations** – Hotelunterkunft für Angehörige, **hospital security** – krankenhauseigenes Sicherheits-/Bewachungssystem, **gift shop** – Einkaufsladen, **financial counseling** – finanzielle Beratung, **medical bill** – Krankenhausrechnung, **discharge** – Entlassung, **advance directives** – vorsorgliche Anweisungen, **to refuse** – ablehnen, **to prolong** – verlängern, **living will** – Patientenerklärung, **inability** – Unfähigkeit, **responsibility** – Verantwortung

3.5.1.1 Your Rights

It is the policy of Cedars Medical Center to affirm the basic rights of human beings for freedom of expression, decision making and action, in our concern for personal dignity in human relationsships.
It is our responsibility to assure that these rights are reserved for all patients, including pediatric, adolescent patients, their parents and/or guardian.

1. **Access to Care:** You shall be accorded impartial access to treatment or accommodations that are available or medically indicated, regardles of race, creed, sex, national origin, religion, handicap or sources of payment for care.
2. **Respect and Dignity:** You have the right to considerate, respectful care at all times and under all circumstances, with recognition of your individual dignity and with protection of your need for privacy.
3. **Privacy and Confidentiality:** You have the right, within the law, to personal and informational privacy, as manifested by the right:
   - To refuse to talk with or see anyone not officially connected with the hospital, including visitors or persons officially connected with the hospital but who are not directly involved in your care.
   - To wear appropriate personal clothing and religious or other symbolic items, aslong as they do not interfer with diagnostic procedures or treatment.
   - To be interviewed and examined in sourroundings designated to assure reasonable privacy. This includes the right to have someone of your own sex present during certain parts of a physical examination, treatment or procedure performed by a health professional of the opposite sex; and the right not to remain disrobed any longer than is required to accomplish the medical purpose for which you were asked to disrobe.
   - To expect that any discussion or consultation involving your case will be conducted discreetly, and that the individuals not directly involved in your care will not be present without your permission.

policy – Leitlinie, **to affirm** – bekräftigen, **basic rights of human beings** – menschliche Grundrechte, **freedom of expression** – Meinungsfreiheit, **decision making** – Entscheidung treffen, **concern** – Sorge, **personal dignity** – persönliche Würde, **human relationships** – menschliche Beziehungen, **reserved** – vorbehalten, **adolescent** – Jugendliche **guardian** – Vormund, **impartial access** – unparteiischen Zugang, **to accord** – bewilligen, **accommodations** – Unterbringung, **available** – vorhanden, **medically indicated** – medizinisch notwendig, **regardless** – ungeachtet, **race** – Rasse, **creed** – Weltanschauung, **national origin** – nationale Herkunft, **handicap** – Behinderung, **sources of payment** – Bezahlungsmodus, **considerate** – fürsorglich, **at all times** – immer, **all circumstances** – allen Umständen, **recognition** – Anerkennung, **dignity** – Würde, **protection** – Schutz, **privacy** – Privatheit, **confidentiality** – Vertraulichkeit, **officially connected** – offiziell verbunden, **involved** – befasst, **interfer** – beeinträchtigen, **surroundings** – Umfeld, **reasonable privacy** – angemessene Privatheit, **someone of your own sex** – eine Person des eigenen Geschlechts, **physical examination** – körperliche Untersuchung, **to perform** – durchführen, **health professional of the opposite sex** – professionelle Person des anderen Geschlechts, **disrobed** – ausgezogen, **involving your case** – ihren Fall betreffend, **to conduct descreetly** – vertraulich führen, **permission** – Erlaubnis

- To have your medical record read only by individuals directly involved in your treatment or in the monitoring and evaluation of your care or charges. Other individuals may have access only with your written authorization or that of your legally authorized representative.
- To expect all communications and other records pertaining to your care, including source of payment for treatment, to be treated as confidential.
- To request a transfer to another room if another patient or visitors in that room are unreasonably disturbing you.
- To be placed in protective privacy when considered necessary for your personal safety.

4. **Personal Safety:** You have the right to expect reasonable safety concerning our practices and environment.
5. **Identity:** You have the right to know the name of individuals providing service to you, and to know which physician or other practitioner is primarily responsible for your care. This includes your right to know of the existence of any professional connection to any other health care or educational institutions involved in your care. Your participation in clinical training programs or in the gathering of data for research purposes shall be voluntary.
6. **Information:** You have the right to obtain from the practitioner responsible for coordinating your care, complete and current information concerning your diagnosis, treatment and any prognosis. This information should be communicated in terms you can reasonably be expected to understand. When it is not medically advisable to give you such information, the information should be made available to a legally authorized individual. You have the right to refuse the passing on of this information.
7. **Communication:** You have the right of access to people outside the hospital by means of visitors and by verbal and written communication. When you do not speak the predominant language of the community, you should have access to an interpreter if we have one readily available.
8. Consent: You or your legally authorized representative have the right to reasonably informed participation in decisions involving your health care, including a prompt response to questions and requests. To the degree possible, this should be based on a

medical record – Patientenakte, **care** – Behandlung, **charges** – Behandlungskosten, **access** – Zugang, **legally authorized representative** – rechtlich autorisierter Vertreter, **records** – Befunde, **pertaining** – bezüglich, **confidential** – vertraulich, **transfer** – Verlegung, **unreasonably disturbing** – unzumutbar störend, **protective privacy** – Isolierung, **practices** – Arbeitsweisen, **providing service** – Leistungen erbringen, **practitioner** – professionelle Person, **primarily responsible** – primär verantwortlich, **existence of professional connection** – Bestehen professioneller Verbindung, **research purposes** – Forschungszwecke, **to obtain** – erhalten, **practitioner responsible** – verantwortlicher Arzt, **current** – aktuell, **should be communicated** – sollte mitgeteilt werden, **in terms** – durch einen Sprachgebrauch, **you can reasonably be expected to understand** – bei dem ein Verständnis Ihrerseits vorausgesetzt werden kann, **advisable** – ratsam, **legally authorized** – rechtlich autorisiert, **the passing on** – Weitergabe, **access** – Verbindung, **predominant** – vorherrschend, **readily available** – leicht verfügbar, **consent** – Einwilligung, **reasonably informed participation** – angemessen informierter Teilnahme, **decisions** – Entscheidungen, **prompt response** – umgehende Antwort

clear, concise explanation of your condition and of all proposed technical procedures, including the possibilities of any risk of mortality or serious side effects, problems related to recuperation, and probability of success. You should not be subjected to any procedure without your voluntary, competent and understanding consent, or that of your legally authorized representative.
Where medically significant alternatives for care or treatment exist, you shall be so informed.
You have the right to know who is responsible for authorizing or performing the procedures or treatment.
You shall be informed if we propose to engage in or perform human experimentation or other research/educational projects affecting your care or treatment and you have the right to refuse to participate in any such activity.

9. **Consultation:** You have the right, at your own request and expense, to consult with a specialist.
10. **Refusal of Treatment:** You may refuse treatment to the extent permitted by the law. When refusal of treatment by you or your legally authorized representative prevents the provision of appropriate care in accordance with ethical and professional standards, the relationship with you may be terminated upon reasonable notice.
11. **Transfer and Continuity of Care:** You may not be transferred to another facility unless you have received a complete explanation of the need for the transfer and the alternatives to such a transfer, and unless the transfer is acceptable to the other facility. You have the right to be informed by the responsible practitioner or his/her delegate of any continuing health care requirements following discharge from the hospital.
12. **Hospital Charges:** Regardless of the source of payment for your care, you have the right to request and receive an itemized and detailed explanation of your total bill for services rendered in our hospital. You have the right to timely notice prior to termination of your eligibility for reimbursement by any third party payor. In addition, you have the right

concise explanation – präzise Erklärung, **condition** – Zustand, **to propose** – vorschlagen, **serious side effects** – ernsthafte Nebenwirkungen, **recuperation** – Gesundung, **probability of success** – Wahrscheinlichkeit des Erfolgs, **to be subjected** – unterzogen werden, **understanding consent** – verstehende Einwilligung, **medically significant** – medizinisch bedeutende, **propose to engage** – vorschlagen teilzunehmen, **research/educational projects** – Forschungs-/Ausbildungsprojekte, **to affect** – betreffen, **your own request** – eigene Anforderung, **expense** – Kosten, **to consult** – konsultieren, **to refuse treatment** – Behandlung verweigern, **extent permitted by law** – im gesetzlich erlaubten Ausmaß, **provision of appropriate care** – Erbringung angemessener Behandlung, **in accordance** – im Einklang, **relationship** – Verhältnis, **to terminate** – auflösen, **reasonable notice** – angemessene Benachrichtigung, **explanation** – Erklärung, **transfer** – Verlegung, **delegate** – Vertreter, **health care requirements** – gesundheitliche Erfordernisse, **regardless of the source of payment** – ungeachtet des Kostenträgers, **itemized and detailed explanation** – dezidierte und detaillierte Erklärung, **services rendered** – erbrachte Leistungen, **timely notice** – rechtzeitige Benachrichtigung, **termination of your eligibility for reimbursement** – vor Ablauf ihres Anspruchs auf Kostenerstattung, **third party payor** – Versicherung

to be given, upon request, full information and necessary counseling on the availability of known financial resources for your care; to know, upon request, and in advance of treatment, whether the health care provider or health care facility accepts the Medicare assignment rate (see Chapter 2, Health Care Insurance); to receive, upon request, prior to treatment, a reasonable estimate of charges for medical care.

13. **Hospital Rules and Regulations:** You shall be informed of our rules and regulations applicable to your conduct as a patient. You are entitled to information about our mechanism for the initiation, review and resolution of your complaints.
14. **Complaints:** You have the right to complain without fear that it will compromise your care or future access to care. To make a complaint, ask an employee for assistance or contact the consumer relations coordinator at 325-5943.

3.5.1.2 Your Responsibilities

1. **Provision of Information:** You have the responsibility to provide, to the best of your knowledge, accurate and complete information about present complaints, past illnesses, hospitalizations, medications, and other matters relating to your health. You have the responsibility to report unexpected changes in your condition to the responsible practitioner. You are responsible for making it known whether you clearly comprehend a contemplated course of action and what is expected of you.
2. Compliance **with Instructions:** You are responsible for following the treatment plan recommended by the practitioner primarily responsible for your care. This may include following instructions of nurses and allied health personnel as they carry out the coordinated plan of care and implement the responsible practitioner's orders and as they enforce our applicable rules and regulations. You are responsible for keeping appointments and, when you are unable to do so for any reason, for notifying the responsible practitioner.
3. **Refusal of Treatment:** You are responsible for your actions if you refuse treatment or do not follow your practitioner's instructions.

upon request – auf Anforderung, **counseling** – Beratung, **availability of known financial resources** – Verfügbarkeit bekannter finanzieller Mittel, **in advance of treatment** – vor der Behandlung, **Medicare assignment rate** – Medicare-Kostenerstattungsrate, **reasonable estimate of charges** – angemessener Kostenvoranschlag, **rules and regulations** – Regeln und Vorschriften, **applicable to your conduct** – Ihr Verhalten betreffend, **initiation** – Einleitung, **review** – Überprüfung, **resolution** – Bearbeitung, **complaints** – Beschwerden, **to complain** – sich beschweren, **to compromise** – beeinträchtigen, **consumer relations coordinator** – Koordinator der hausinternen Patientenanlaufstelle, **the best of your knowledge** – nach bestem Wissen, **present complaints** – derzeitige Beschwerden, **past illnesses** – frühere Erkrankungen, **hospitalizations** – Krankenhausaufenthalte, **to report** – berichten, **unexpected changes in your condition** – unerwartete Veränderungen Ihres Zustandes, **to comprehend** – verstehen, **contemplated course of action** – überlegter Behandlungsplan, **compliance** – mitmachen, **to recommend** – empfehlen, **practitioner primarily responsible** – primär verantwortliche Arzt, **practitioner's orders** – ärztliche Verordnungen, **to enforce** – durchsetzen, **appointments** – Termine, **to notify** – benachrichtigen, **refuse** – verweigern

3

2:00 PM
Cedars in the News #2

Solon Gray shows you how the physicians and surgeons at Cedars Medical Center treat cancer. Learn what microsurgery can do. Excerpted from local TV news, this program covers the Cedars cholesterol program, which tests local blood donors' cholesterol levels for free.

2:15 PM
How to Beat Cancer

An interesting and informative program describing various types of cancer, its causes and ways to avoid it. Originally broadcast on WTVJ-TV, Channel 4.

3:10 PM
Dietary Management of Fat and Cholesterol

This program explains the relationship between saturated fat, cholesterol and heart disease. Food preparation tips that reduce fat content and the special problems of eating out are discussed.

3:20 PM
Type II Diabetes

This program examines the ways in which Type II diabetes can be controlled. Changes in lifestyle and diet necessary to control this disease and allow an individual to lead a healthy life are described.

3:30 PM
The Sugar Film

An "awareness" program. This film deals with the effects of sugar in the body, and creates an awareness of just how much sugar the average American consumes (139 lbs. a year!) and discusses the importance of reading labels for "hidden" sugars.

4:00 PM
For Our Patients

Watch this show as you read your "For Our Patients" handbook. This program and booklet will give you a better idea of what to expect during your hospital stay at Cedars.

4:10 PM
Before and After Your Surgery

This program provides a better understanding of what to expect before and after surgery. Nursing care, medication, recovery room and exercises are discussed.

4:25 PM
Understanding Your Anesthesia

Learn more about a technique used to control pain during an operation. This program explains various types of anesthesia and how they are used.

Fig. 3: Cedars in-house Television Program for Patients, Cedars Medical Center, Miami, Florida.

4. **Hospital Charges:** You are responsible for assuring that the financial obligations of your health care are fulfilled as promptly as possible.
5. **Hospital Rules and Regulations:** You are responsible for following hospital rules and regulations affecting patient care and conduct, including the »No Smoking« policy.
6. **Respect and Consideration:** You are responsible for being considerate of the rights of other patients and hospital personnel, and for assisting in the control of noise and the number of visitors. You are responsible for being respectful of the property of other persons and of the hospital.
7. **Complaints:** You have the responsibility to make complaints and constructive criticism known to our management so that we can be aware and act accordingly.

This written information given to patients on admission and, in my practical experience of many years, its content being carried out in daily practice by the hospital personnel shows the attention paid to patients and clearly reflects the philosophy of the hospital (see this Chapter, Philosophy).

In addition to receiving the information booklet patients can obtain a variety of information via the special in-house television channel for patients. Using the printed in-house television program they are able to choose films they are interested in. Fig. 3 shows a sample page of the in-house television program.

3.6 Medical Ethics Commission

The work of a Medical Ethics Commission is concerned with moral issues arising during the treatment and care of patients. Following, an overview is given of the functioning of a Medical Ethics Committee by presenting excerpts taken from the administration manual of St. John's Hospital in Springfield, Illinois. In the St. John's Hospital this commission is named Medical Moral Committee.

3.6.1 Purpose

- To serve as a resource to those who wish to consult about medical moral issues of patient care.
- To provide a forum for interdisciplinary dialogue on medical moral issues arising in thehospital.

financial obligations – finanzielle Verpflichtungen, **prompt** – umgehend, **conduct** – Verhaltensweise, **consideration** – Rücksichtnahme, **to be considerate** – rücksichtsvoll sein, **property** – Eigentum, **complaints** – Beschwerden, **be aware** – wissen, **act accordingly** – entsprechend handeln, **practical experience** – praktische Erfahrung, **content** – Inhalt, **to carry out** – durchführen, **attention paid** – Aufmerksamkeit gegeben, **variety** – Vielfalt, **sample** – Muster, **Medical Ethics Commission** – medizinische Ethik-Kommission, **concerned** – besorgt sein, **moral issues** – moralische Aspekte, **manual** – Handbuch, **to serve** – dienen, **patient care** – Patientenversorgung

- To review, develop, and recommend hospital policies and procedures in light of their moral appropriateness.
- To review and discuss medical moral literature for self-education and to recommend educational opportunities in the area of medical moral questions for board, medical staff, personnel, patients and their families and community.
- To monitor legislation and relevant legal proceedings which may have medical legal implications.

3.6.2 Membership

Efforts should be made to gain diversity of competence and experience. The following categories of persons should be represented:

- Administration,
- Other Health Care Staff,
- Medical Staff,
- Nursing Staff,
- Medical Student,
- Catholic Theologian with Medical Moral Background,
- Consumer.

All members are required to study materials on the committee resource list so that all come to the meetings with a common educational basis.
The Committee meets monthly and more often, as needed, to address special issues.

3.6.3 Requesting a Consult

A request for a consult may be made by anyone who perceives there may be an ethical dilemma in making a health care decision.
Committee members can be contacted by using certain phone/page numbers availabe in all hospital departments.

Requests can be made in the following manner:

- Medical staff can order the consultation directly,
- Hospital staff may request a consultation directly or through their managers,
- The patient and/or family, guardian or others may request a consultation directly or through hospital staff.

to review – überprüfen, **to develop** – entwickeln, **policies and procedures** – Leitlinien und Standards, **appropriateness** – Angemessenheit, **opportunities** – Möglichkeiten, **board** – Aufsichtsrat, **staff** – Personal, **legislation** – Gesetzgebung, **legal proceedings** – rechtliche Verfahren, **implications** – Auswirkungen, **membership** – Mitgliedschaft, **diversity** – Vielseitigkeit, **to represent** – vertreten, **consumer** – Verbraucher, **common educational basis** – einheitlichen Wissensgrundlage, **issues** – Aspekte, **to request** – anfordern, **to perceive** – wahrnehmen, **members** – Mitglieder, **to order** – verordnen, **hospital staff** – Krankenhausmitarbeiter

3.6.4 Consultation Process

- The chairperson or secretary of the Medical Moral Committee, or the hospital medical director are notified of the request.
- The person notified assumes responsibility for coordinating the consultation process.
- The coordinator of the consultation process discusses the request with the attending physician.
- Pertinent data are collected i.e. summary review of the chart (see chapter 5, The Chart), discussion with appropriate hospital staff, and literature search as indicated.

It may be necessary to:

- interview the patient, family, guardian or others to determine their understanding of the patient's condition and treatment options,
- set up a meeting of the Medical Moral Committee.

Recommendations of the Medical Moral Committee as formulated by the involved committee members are documented and signed by at least three committee members. The completed report is placed in the patient's chart and a copy is filed with administrative records. The committee member having coordinated the consultation shall follow up and review the case as necessary. If indicated, the case will be discussed at the monthly Committee meeting. The final outcome will be reported to the committee by the committee member attending to the case.

3.7 A Quality Controlling Agency

Hospitals are licensed by the state in which they are established and must meet given quality standards. There are state and private controlling agencies ensuring a certain level of quality of health care delivered by hospitals and other health care facilities. Following, the best known quality controlling agency is introduced.

3.7.1 The Joint Commission on the Accreditation of Health Care Organizations

By far the most important of the controlling agencies is the JOINT COMMISSION ON THE ACCREDITATION OF HEALTH CARE ORGANIZATIONS – JCAHO, commonly called THE JOINT COMMISSION. The Joint Commission with head quarters in Oakbrook, Illinois, was founded in 1918 by a group of surgeons with the purpose to ensure high quality standards of the work of this group of medical specialists. Today the Joint Commission is a highly regarded quality assurance agency which inspects hospitals and other

chairperson – Vorsitzender, **to assume responsibility** – Verantwortung übernehmen, **attending physician** – behandelnde Arzt, **pertinent data** – fallbezogene Unterlagen, **appropriate hospital staff** – entsprechende Krankenhausmitarbeiter, **search** – suchen, **condition** – Zustand, **treatment options** – Behandlungsmöglichkeiten, **recommendations** – Empfehlungen, **final outcome** – Endergebnis, **to file** – ablegen, **agency** – agentur, **to licence** – genehmigen, **to ensure** – sicherstellen, **to found** – gründen, **surgeons** – Chirurgen, **highly-regarded** – hoch angesehen

health care facilities nationwide every three years using standardized quality citeria. The health care facilities which fulfill the required quality criteria are accredited by the Joint Commission for three years at which time the process is repeated.

3.7.1.1 Mission

The self-declared mission of the Joint Commission as stated in the accreditation manual reads as follows: »*The mission of the Joint Commission on the Accreditation of Health Care Organizations is to improve the quality of health care provided to the public. The Joint Commission develops standards of quality in collaboration with health professionals and others and stimulates health care organizations to meet or exceed the standards through accreditation and the teaching of quality improvement standards*« (Joint Commission, 1991).

The voluntary participation of health care facilities in this accreditation process has to do with the fact that accreditation enhances reimbursement by private and governmental health insurance carriers. Furthermore, it is important for the administration of health care facilities to know about currently existing quality levels, based on the determined criteria of the Joint Commission, in order to eliminate quality deficits and thus maintain defined quality levels. And finally,accreditation constitutes official confirmation that the particular health care institution is delivering a standard of patient care approved by JCAHO and on par with other nationally recognized institutions.

3.7.1.2 Controlling Process

The process of accreditation is carried out by an expert team consisting of a hospital administrator, a physician and a registered nurse. The process lasts, depending on the size of a health care facility, from 1-3 or more days and includes all departments. This means that not only Physician Services, Patient Services and Nursing Services are investigated, but also the support departments Support A, Support B Support C, as well as Human Resources, Finance and Administration are inspected (see the Organization Chart, Fig. 4, Seite 51). On the basis of the quality criteria listed in the different departments' specific standards it is determined by the inspectors to which degree the criteria of a particular standard are met. Failure to meet the criteria results in, depending on the gravity of the deficit, oral or written reprimands by the commissioners. Deficits have to be corrected within a given time period and a written report has to be submitted to head quarters showing the improvement. If certain deficits are not corrected within the given time a partial accreditation is issued. In a worst case scenario no accreditation is given. This can entail the refusal of the health care

health care facilities – Gesundheitseinrichtungen, **to repeat** – wiederholen, **accreditation manual** – Zertifizierungshandbuch, **mission** – Aufgabe, **voluntary participation** – freiwillige Teilnahme, **reimbursement** – Kostenerstattung, **governmental** – staatlich, **health insurance carriers** – Krankenversicherungen, **currently existing quality levels** – derzeit bestehendes Qualitätsniveau, **constitutes official confirmation** – bedeuted offizielle Bestätigung, **on par** – gleichwertig, **hospital administrator** – Krankenhausbetriebswirt, **degree** – Grad, **failure** – Nichteinhalten, **gravity** – Schwere, **reprimands** – Beanstandungen, **partial** – teilweise, **a worst case scenario** – im schlimmsten Fall, **refusal** – Verweigerung

insurance companies to do business with this particular health care provider and as a result of this the closing of the facility (for additional information on the Joint Commission in German see: Kellnhauser 1991/1992).

3.8 Excursion: »Care« and »Clinical«

Das Wort **CARE** beinhaltet zahlreiche semantische Variationen. Folglich kann eine **sinngemäße Interpretation** von Care nur im Zusammenhang mit dem jeweiligen Kontext erfolgen. Nachstehend werden Beispiele des unterschiedlichen kontextuellen Einsatzes von CARE unter drei verschiedenen Aspekten aufgezeigt.

1. Persönlicher Aspekt:

Care	Fürsorglichkeit, Hilfestellung
I care	Es bedeutet mir etwas Es ist mir wichtig Ich nehme Anteil
I care about you	Du bedeutest mir etwas Ich mag Dich
I take care of you	Ich versorge Dich Ich pflege Dich Ich stehe Dir bei
To take care	Vorsichtig sein

2. Pflegerischer Aspekt:

To give care	Pflegen, Behandeln
Nursing Care	Pflege
I care about the patient	Der Patient ist mir wichtig
I take care of the patient	Ich pflege den Patienten

3. Institutioneller Aspekt:

Health Care Politics	Gesundheitspolitik
Health Care Systems	Gesundheitssysteme
Health Care Services	Gesundheitsversorgung, Gesundheitsdienste
Health Care Providers	Gesundheitseinrichtungen, Leistungserbringer
Medical Care	Medizinische Behandlung
Patient Care	Patientenversorgung
A Caring Environment	Ein menschlich fürsorgliches Umfeld

Durch Aufzeigen dieser Beispiele ist der sprachliche Einsatz des Wortes CARE bei weitem nicht erschöpft. Es soll lediglich eine Vorstellung darüber vermittelt werden, wie vielseitig dieses Wort Verwendung findet und wie wichtig es deshalb ist, dieses Wort im inhaltlichen Zusammenhang zu verstehen, um bestimmte Texte entsprechend interpretieren zu können.

Das Wort **CLINICAL** wird in den verschiedensten Konstellationen gebraucht und kann leicht missverstanden werden.
Grundsätzlich bedeutet clinical für die Pflege: »**Hands on the patient.**« Das heißt: direktes Arbeiten mit und am Patienten.

Entsprechend bedeutet **clinical nursing** – pflegerisches Arbeiten am Bett.

Die nachstehenden Beispiele zeigen die Nutzung des Wortes **clinical** im kontextuellen Zusammenhang:

- This teaching unit includes theoretical and clinical aspects.
- The clinical work of this nurse is excellent.
- Results of nursing research must be integrated in clinical practice.

4 The Nursing Department

In diesem Kapitel wird die Abteilung des Pflegedienstes beschrieben. Anhand eines Organigramms wird beispielhaft die Organisationsstruktur eines Pflegedienstes aufgezeigt. Das pflegerische Selbstverständnis und das damit einhergehende Leitbild des Pflegedienstes wird vorgestellt. Es werden die Stellung und Aufgaben sowie die erforderliche Qualifikation der Direktorin des Pflegedienstes illustriert. Es wird der Einfluss bestimmter pflegerischer Selbstverwaltungsorganisationen sowie der einer ausserbetrieblichen Kontroll-Kommission auf die Sicherstellung der Pflegequalität verdeutlicht. Es wird der für alle pflegerischen Mitarbeiter gültige ethische Kodex aufgeführt. Auf die in der Abteilung Pflegedienst vorhandenen unterschiedlichen Positionen wird eingegangen. Die Ziele und Hauptaufgaben der Innerbetrieblichen Fortbildungsabteilung werden skizziert.

4.1 Organization

The nursing department has a written organization plan. This plan is part of the overall organization plan of the hospital (see Chapter 3, Hospital Organization Chart) In general, the nursing department organization charts of American hospitals are similar to the one displayed in Figure 4. It shows the different nursing positions and indicates the lines of responsibility.

Looking at the nursing organization chart from the top down you see the **Director of Nurses.** The next position to the side is the **Secretary**, followed by the **Assistant Director** = Stellvertretung.

Following the horizontal line from left to right, you see the position of the **Quality Assurance Coordinator**, next on the same line the **DRG Coordinator**, next to it the **Nursing Supervisors** = Abteilungsleitungen,* next is the **Infection Control Coordinator** = Hygieneschwester, the vertical line shows the **Central Supply** = Pflegematerial-Ausgabe; further on the horizontal line, you find the **Inservice Coordinators** = Pflegelehrpersonen der Innerbetrieblichen Fortbildung, and the **Supervisor of Surgery** = Abteilungsleitung der Operationsabteilung.

The last vertical line shows the Supervisor of Surgery who is the superior of the **Head Nurse of the Surgical Recovery Room** = Stationsleitung chirurgischer Aufwachraum, the **Charge Nurse** = deren Vertretung, the **RN Staff** = examinierte Schwestern/Pfleger der Operations-

* Im englischen Sprachgebrauch ist ein Supervisor eine Fachvorgesetzte. Der im deutschen Sprachgebrauch übliche Supervisor ist im englischen ein »psychological counselor«.

to display – darstellen, **to indicate** – aufzeigen, **responsibility** – Verantwortung, **overall** – gesamt, **organization chart** – Organigramm

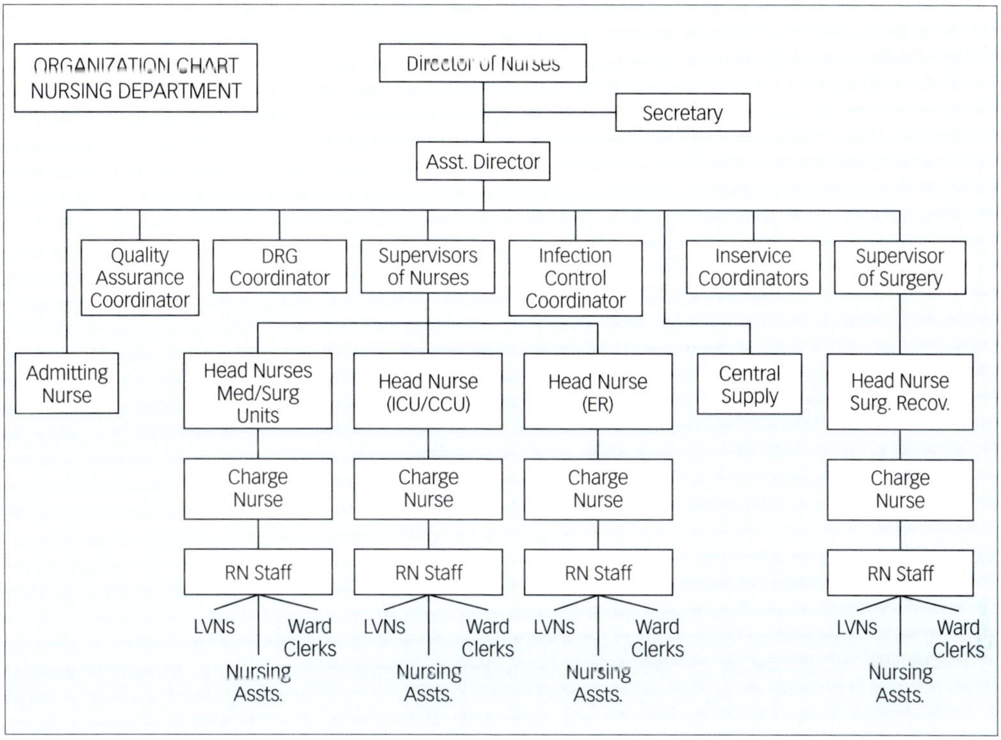

Fig. 4: Organization chart nursing department (ROWLAND and ROWLAND 1992 – revised by the author).

abteilung, the **Surgical Technicians** = Operationsassistenten, **Nursing Assistants** = Pflegehelferinnen, and the **Surgical Clerk** = Sekretärin der Operationsabteilung.

The vertical line on the far left, shows the **Admitting Nurse** = Aufnahmeschwester. In the next three columns to the right, you see on top **Head Nurses Medical/Surgical Units** = Stationsschestern der medizinischen/chirurgischen Stationen, **Head Nurse Intensive Care Unit/Cardiac Care Unit** = Stationsschwester Intensivabteilung/Kardiologische Intensivabteilung and **Head Nurse Emergency Room** = Stationsschwester Notfallabteilung.

These head nurses are responsible for the following categories of nursing personnel:
The **Charge Nurse** = stellvertretende Stationsschwester, the **RN Staff*** = Krankenschwestern, the **LVNs** = Licensed Vocational Nurses, also called **LPNs,** Licensed Practical Nurses = examinierte Pflegehelferinnen, **Nursing Assistants** = Pflegehelferinnen, **Ward Clerks,** also called **Unit Secretaries** = Stationssekretärinnen.

* Für eine Aufgabenbeschreibung der RN = Examinierte Schwester in deutsch siehe Kellnhauser E.: Krankenpflege in den USA. In: Die Schwester, Der Pfleger, Melsungen, 8/1988.

to call – nennen

4.2 Mission Statement

The mission statement of the nursing department declares the reason for the existence of the nursing service department. It describes how the nursing department sees itself and what it aims to accomplish. It is nursing's commitment to a specific purpose or mission.The mission statement exists in written form. It is revised as changes in service occur.

A mission statement for the department of nursing may read as follows:
»*The Nursing Service exists to provide quality patient care; and to collaborate with the medical staff, coworkers, and other allied professionals in our pursuit of excellence.* These collaborative efforts will include continuous quality improvement, education, and research activities in the health care continuum« *(Mission Statement, Department of Nursing, Nursing Orientation Manual, Cedars Medical Center, Miami,* Florida, 1998*)*.

4.3 Philosophy

The written philosophy of nursing describes the vision, the spiritual values of the department of nursing. It declares the humanistic attitudes of nursing. It is the idiological guide for all planning and delivery of nursing care. Like the mission statement the philosophy exists inwritten form. Both, the mission statement and the philosophy of nursing are in accordance with the philosophy of the hospital.
Following, is the Philosophy of Nursing at Cedars Medical Center, Miami, Florida, 1998:

»WE BELIEVE that each member of the Nursing Services Department of Cedars Medical Center has the responsibility to pursue excellence in the delivery of nursing care. Registered nurses are responsible and accountable for defining, delegating, and coordinating nursing care provided throughout the facility.
In order to achieve this excellence, we support the standards of care that apply to all settings in which nursing care is provided by the hospital.

WE ARE DEDICATED to providing quality, humanistic, cost-effective care to all patients and their families.

WE SUPPORT professional growth through a variety of avenues including the promotion of career ladders (see chapter 6, Professional Opportunity) and continuing education.

aims to accomplish – anstrebt zu erzielen, **commitment** – Verpflichtung, **to revise** – überarbeiten, **collaborate** – mitarbeiten, **allied professionals** – relevante Heilberufe, **pursuit** – Bestreben, **effort** – Bemühen, **improvement** – Verbesserung, **philosophy** – Leitlinie, **spiritual values** – geistige Werte, **guide** – Richtschnur, **accordance** – Einklang, **to believe** – glauben, **responsibility** – Verantwortung, **to persue** – streben nach, **delivery of nursing care** – Durchführung von Pflege, **accountable** – nachweispflichtig, **facility** – Einrichtung, **apply to all settings** – beziehen auf alle Bereiche, **to be dedicated** – verpflichtet sein, **professional growth** – professionelles Wachsen, **variety of avenues** – unterschiedliche Weise, **promotion of career ladders** – Förderung von Karriereleitern, **continuing education** – innerbetriebliche Fortbildung

WE BELIEVE that all members of the health care team must work together in order to meet the needs of the patients and their families.

WE BELIEVE it is our responsibility to provide an environment which is conducive to the restauration of health or to a peaceful death of patients by treating patients and families with respect and dignity.

WE SUPPORT our professional and social commitment to the community through ongoing efforts to increase public awareness about health issues and the role that the nursing profession plays in health maintenance and/or restauration; and by participating in activities which contribute towards the achievement of community health goals.«

Both, the mission statement and the philosophy of nursing are printed in the Nursing Orientation Handbook (see chapter 6, Nursing Orientation). Both are discussed with new nursing employees during the time of orientation. They are expected to live these ideals in their every day work and to show this in the way they interact with, treat and care for patients. (For a detailed description of a philosophy of nursing in German see *Kellnhauser* in: Thiemes Pflege 2000: 121.)

4.4 The Director of Nursing

The Director of Nursing manages and is responsible for the department of nursing.

4.4.1 Title

Different titles are used for the position of Director of Nursing. The most frequently used are: Director of Nursing, Nursing Service Director, Chief Nurse, Associate Director Department of Nursing, Vice President for Patient Services. These different titles are adaptations from similar titles existing for persons in similar positions in other departments of the hospital.

4.4.2 Position in the Organizational Structure

The position of the department of nursing, and with it the director of nursing, relativ to the total organizational structur is shown in the Organization Chart of the hospital (see chapter 3, Hospital Organization) Since the Executive Director = the CEO carries the sole responsibility for the functioning of the hospital there is no tripartite form of hospital administration. Consequently, the Director of Nursing is not on the same level as the CEO in the organization. This is not to say that there is not close collaboration between the two.

to meet – erfüllen, **environment** – Umfeld, **conducive** – fördernd, **dignity** – Würde, **ongoing** – fortwährende, **efforts** – fortwährende Anstrengungen, **public awareness** – das öffentliche Bewusstsein, **health issues** – gesundheitliche Aspekte, **restauration** – Wiederherstellung, **to contribute** – beitragen, **achievement** – Erreichung, **community health goals** – Gesundheitsziele der Gemeinde, **to discuss** – besprechen, **nursing employees** – Pflegepersonal, **orientation** – Einführung, **to be responsible** – verantwortlich sein, **frequently** – häufig, **adaptation** – Anpassung, **relativ** – im Verhältnis, **CEO – chief executive officer** – Betriebsleiter, **tripartite** – dreiteilig

Since all categories of personnel working in a hospital have written position descriptions, also called job descriptions, there is also a position description for the Director of Nursing. Following, are excerpts from the position description for the Director of Nursing at St. John's Hospital in Springfield, Illinois, modified by the author.

4.4.3 Purpose of the Position

Provides administrative leadership for the Nursing Service Division and for coordinating and directing all nursing activities toward common hospital goals.

4.4.3.1 Management

Provides leadership by integrating the organization's philosophy and values into daily activities as well as future planning.

Dedicates management efforts toward collaboration, innovation and enabling others to perform effectively by using a systems approach for continual improvement.

Participates with leaders of the governing body, hospital managers, medical staff and other clinical leaders in the decision-making process of the hospital.

Formulates long-range objectives, plans and programs for the nursing devision, integrating those with hospital goals.

Develops goals and provides for ongoing monitoring of the nursing division's performance in the following areas: patient care, customer satisfaction, employee performance, recruitment and retention, staffing, staff development, physician relations, interdepartmental relations, employee health and safety, and infection control measures.

Participates in the hospital's provision of continuous quality improvement.

position descriptions – Tätigkeitsbeschreibungen, **to modify** – überarbeiten, **purpose** – Zweck, **administrative leadership** – betriebliche Führung, **common** – gemeinsam, **to integrate** – einfügen, **values** – Werte, **to dedicate** – sich für etwas einsetzen, **to enable** – befähigen, **systems approach** – systematische Herangehensweise, **governing body** – Verwaltungsrat, **medical staff** – Ärzteschaft, **decision making process** – Entscheidungsfindungsprozess, **long range objectives** – Langzeitziele, **nursing devision's performance** – Leistungen des Pflegedienstes, **customer satisfaction** – Kundenzufriedenheit, **employee performance** – Leistung der Mitarbeiter, **recruitment and retention** – Personalgewinnung- und erhalt, **staffing** – Personalzuteilung, **staff development** – Personalentwicklung, **physician relations** – Beziehung zu Ärzten, **interdepartmental relations** – Beziehungen zu anderen Abteilungen, **employee health and safety** – Mitarbeitergesundheit- und sicherheit, **infection control measures** – Hygienemaßnahmen, **provision** – Verfügbarmachung

Provides leadership in assuring compliance with all licensing and accrediting agencies' regulations/requirements; (see chapter 3, Joint Commission, chapter 4, Licensures) maintains systems of clinical and administrative records and reports to satisfy those agencies, and submits an information base for effective administrative action.

4.4.3.2 Nursing

Develops patient care programs, policies and procedures that determine how the nursing care needs of patients are assessed, met and evaluated.

Provides for the establishment of a caring environment for clinical practice and quality patient care.

Ensures that patient care delivery systems take into consideration patient mix, knowledge and skills of nursing staff, available resources and community needs.

4.4.3.3 Leadership

Provides management counseling and professional development for nursing managers.

Supports the education of nursing students and other hospital-based education activities to maintain an optimal learning environment and to provide appropriate educational experience.

4.4.3.4 Budget

Develops the budget for the division of nursing.

Develops an ongoing monitoring system of the nursing budget throughout the fiscal year.

4.4.3.5 Qualifications

Must possess a current professional licence in this State (see chapter 4, Professional Licensures).

Must possess a masters degree in nursing or a related field (2. Universitätsgrad).

provides leadership – übernimmt die Führung, **compliance** – Mitarbeit, **licensing and accrediting agencies** – Zulassungs- und Anerkennungsbehörden, **clinical and administrative records** – klinische und betriebliche Dokumentation, **reports** – Berichte, **to satisfy** – befriedigen, **care programs** – Pflegeprogramme, **policies and procedures** – Leitlinien und Standards, **nursing care needs** – Pflegebedürfnisse, **to assess** – einschätzen, **met** – erfüllt, **caring environment** – fürsorgliche Atmosphäre, **patient care delivery systems** – Pflegesysteme, **to take into consideration** – berücksichtigen, **patient mix** – Patienten mit unterschiedlichen Krankheitsschweregraden, **knowledge and skills** – Wissen und Fähigkeiten, **nursing staff** – Pflegepersonal, **community needs** – Bedürfnisse in der Gemeinde, **learning environment** – Lernumfeld, **appropriate educational experience** – erforderliche Ausbildungserfahrung, **division of nursing** – der Pflegedienst, **current professional licence** – gültige professionelle Berufserlaubnis, **to possess** – besitzen

Must have a minimum of five years experience in a senior management position with a wide scope of administrative and clinical responsibility.

Generally, position descriptions are revised bi-annually by a committee of nurses designated for this kind of work.

Like the work of all employees of the hospital, the performance of the Director of Nursing too is evaluated annually by her superior on the basis of the position description. Efficient and effective work performance is duely recognized and appropriate new goals are set for the new period to come. In case of poor performance a certain time period for improvement is allowed. If improvement is not forthcoming the Director of Nursing, like any other employee, can expect to lose her position.

4.5 Quality Patient Care

In order to implement the philosophy of nursing into daily nursing practice and thus provide quality patient care, it is the responsibility of the director of nursing to create a framework for the accomplishment of these objectives. The framework for these objectives are the nursing administration standards. The director of nursing has a certain freedom of creativity in establishing these standards. But there are also several external controlling agencies whose established standards must be met. These agencies see to it that their standards are observed. However, they also offer help to nursing departments for setting up specific standards.

To show how the standards of the control agencies affect the management of the nursing department, following below three dominant agencies are selected and **one standard** of each agency is presented.

4.5.1 ANA – American Nurses Association

Standards for Organized Nursing

Standard 1 The division of nursing has a philosophy and structure that ensure the delivery of high quality nursing care and provide means for resolving nursing practice issues throughout the health care organization.

senior management position – gehobener Management Position, **wide scope** – breite Basis, **revised bi-annually** – zweijährlich überarbeitet, **to designate** – beauftragen, **duely** – gebührend, **to recognize** – anerkennen, **poor performance** – mangelhafte Leistung, **improvement** – Verbesserung, **forthcoming** – eintreten, **nursing practice** – Pflegearbeit, **framework** – Rahmenkonzept, **accomplishment** – Erreichung, **objectives** – Ziele, **nursing administration** – Pflegemenagement, **controlling agencies** – Kontrollbehörden, **must be met** – müssen erfüllt werden, **to see to it** – darauf achten, **dominant** – vorherrschend, **nursing care** – Pflege, **to provide means** – Mittel einsetzen, **to resolve** – lösen

Standard 2 The division of nursing is administered by a qualified nurse manager who is a member of the corporate administration.
Standard 3 Policies and practices of the division of nursing provide for equality and continuity of nursing services that recognize cultural, economic, and social differences among patients of the health care organization.
Standard 4 The division of nursing ensures that the nursing process is used to design and provide nursing care to meet the individual needs of patients/clients in the context of their families.
Standard 5 The division of nursing provides an environment that ensures the effectiveness of nursing practice.
Standard 6 The division of nursing ensures the development of educational programs to support the delivery of high quality nursing care.
Standard 7 The division of nursing initiates, utilizes and participates in research studies or projects for the improvement of nursing care (see Rowland and Rowland, 1992, page 124).

4.5.2 JCAHO – Joint Commission for the Accreditation of Health Care Organizations

Vereinigte Kommission zur Akkreditierung von Gesundheitseinrichtungen (see chapter 3, A Quality Controlling Agency).

One of the first items the Joint Commission on their regular inspection visits will want to see are the nursing department's policy and procedure manuals. The emphasis of the inspection is placed on the actuality of the contents in these manuals.

4.5.2.1 Policy and Procedure Manuals

Since there is often confusion about how to differentiate between a policy and a procedure the two items are defined as follows:

Policy – a policy is a declaration of intent, a general overview of what has to be done.
Example: **All patients will receive appropriate skin care.**
In other words: A policy is a guideline for a certain aspect of care.

Procedure – a procedure determines the detailed steps to accomplish the intention set forth in the policy.
Example: **The nursing standard for skin care with its many detailed steps- including bed sore prevention- is utilized for all patients.**

corporate administration – Betriebsleitung, **equality and continuity** – Gleichbehandlung und Kontinuität, **environment** – Umfeld, **to utilize** – nutzen, **policy and procedure manuals** – Handbücher für Leitlinien und Standards, **emphasis** – Hauptgewicht, **actuality of the contents** – Aktualität der Inhalte, **procedure** – standard, **to differentiate** – unterscheiden, **declaration of intent** – Festlegung einer Absicht, **general overview** – allgemeiner Überblick, **to accomplish** (a certain task) – eine bestimmte Tätigkeit durchführen, **to set forth** – festlegen, **bed sore** – Dekubitus, **measurable** – messbar

In other words: A procedure is a nursing standard with measurable criteria.

The nursing service department has policy and procedure manuals. This means that in **every area** where nursing care is given there is a policy and procedure manual, so that nursing personnel has easy access to them. Special care areas have the basic manuals and in addition policies and procedures for their specialized work, i.e. Intensive Care, Dialysis Unit. In some hospitals the policies are kept separately from the procedures in two different ring books. In others policies and procedures are combined in one volume.

Following is an example of a combined version of a policy and a procedure taken from the Policy and Procedure Book of the St. John's Hospital in Springfield, Illinoi, and modified by the author.
The content of this policy and procedure provides a guideline for employees in how to document an interdisciplinary communication or a conference.

4.5.2.2 Departmental Manual

Department: Nursing Services
Subject: Interdisciplinary Collaboration in Patient Care
Policy: Interdisciplinary collaboration is an integral part of patient care.
Purpose: To provide documentation guidelines of interdisciplinary collaboration in patient care.

Procedure:
1. The Interdisciplinary Communication/Conference Form is used to document formal interdisciplinary patient care conferences, as well as informal interdisciplinary communications.
2. The discipline who initiates the communication is responsible for completing the appropriate section of the form.
3. The date, disciplines involved, the description of the patient care need and the appropriate goal/plan are to be included in the documentation. The reader should be referred to the appropriate section of the patient record (i.e. doctors' progress notes, nurses' notes) for the documentation of the intervention and any other pertinent information.
4. Subsequent interdisciplinary conferences/communications are recorded on the same form to maintain continuity and assess progress toward expected outcomes.
5. The form is located in the nurses section of the patient's chart, immediately under the green divider (see chapter 5, The Chart).
6. This form may be utilized in the care of outpatients as well as inpatients.

A specific form for this documentation is available in the different nursing departments.

nursing service department – der Pflegedienst, **nursing personnel** – Pflegepersonal, **easy access** – leichten Zugriff, **special areas** – Spezialeinheiten, **to combine** – zusammenlegen, **content** – Inhalt, **guideline** – Leitfaden, **department manual** – Abteilungs-/Stationshandbuch, **integral part** – wesentlicher Teil, **subject** – Thema, **form** – Formular, **formal** – formal, **discipline** – Fachbereich, **appropriate section** – entprechender Teil, **to refer** – verweisen, **pertinent** – bedeutend

This combined policy and procedure in the category of »interdepartmental cooperation« is **one example** of the numerous policies and procedures existing in the deparment of nursing service with new ones being added continuously. To put them in some manageable order they are divided into three categories:

- Policies and Procedures for General Nursing Service
- Policies and Procedures for Interdepartmental Cooperation
- Policies and Procedures for Specific Nursing Care

At their completion all policies and procedures are signed by the responsible nursing persons, i.e. the director of nursing, nursing supervisors and the education coordinator.
Joint Commission standards require that all policies and procedures are updated at least bi-annually. The date of the revision has to be stated on the document and the update verified by the signature of the director of nursing. A special nursing committee exists which meets regularly, i.e. monthly or bi-monthly in order to keep these policies and procedures current.

4.5.3 State Board of Nursing

Validity of licensures

For the State Board of Nursing quality patient care begins with the fact that all Registered Nurses and Licensed Practical Nurses must hold a valid professional license (see Chapter 1, Licensure).
A professional license is issued by the State Board of Nursing after a nursing person has successfully passed the licensing exams. At the time the nurse receives her professional license her name is admitted to the register, which is the list of nurses allowed to practice professional nursing. With the registration the title RN = Registered Nurse or LPN = Licensed Practical Nurse is bestowed. In the majority of the States the professional license has to be renewed every two years. In order to get the license renewed RNs and LPNs have to attend during the period of the two years 20 hours of continuing education at a teaching institution approved by the State Board. Upon submission of proof of the 20 hours of continuing education to the Board the license will be renewed.

The State Board of Nursing sends a list with the names of all registered nursing personnel to all directors of nursing annually, so that they can check whether every professional nurse on their staff has a current license. In case a nursing person does not possess a current license she can not be allowed to continue working as a professional nurse.This means she has to be demoted in status and salary to a non-professional worker until she has met the requirements set forth by the State Board, and subsequently has obtained her license. No health care facility will employ a nurse without a valid license.

numerous – zahlreich, **completion** – Fertigstellung, **nursing supervisor** – Abteilungsleitung, **to update** – aktualisieren, **revision** – Überarbeitung, **to verify** – bestätigen, **current** – aktuell, **validity of licensures** – Gültigkeit der Berufserlaubnis, **State Board of Nursing** – Pflegekammer, **licencing exams** – Staatsexamen, **registration** – Registrierung, **to bestow** – verleihen, **to renew** – erneuern, **continuing education** – Fortbildung, **submission of proof** – Vorlage des Beweises, **to approve** – anerkennen, **annually** – jährlich, **to demote** – zurückstufen, **set forth** – festgelegt

These examples show, how these external controlling agencies require from nursing management the fulfillment of standards which directly or indirectly affect the quality of patient care. Since these controlling agencies have existed since the early years of the previous century it is not surprising that the number of standards has continually increased and their content has been and is subsequently refined and kept current in the interest of quality patient care.

The aspect of cooperation between quality control agencies is examplified by the fact that the nursing person of the Joint Commision checks the list of valid licensures during the Commision's control visits.

4.6 Nursing Ethics

The department of nursing maintains an ethical code for all its employees. This code is in conformity with the one ssued by the American Nurses Association – ANA, and is in accordance with the professional codex established by the International Council of Nursing – ICN. Following is an abbreviated form of this code.

4.6.1 Ethical Code for Nurses

1. The nurse provides services with respect for human dignity and the uniqueness of the client unrestricted by considerations of social or economic status, personal attributes, or the nature of health problems.
2. The nurse acts to safeguard the client's right to privacy by judiciously protecting information of a confidential nature.
3. The nurse acts to safeguard the client and the public when health care and safety are affected by the incompetent, unethical or illegal practice of any person.
4. The nurse assumes responsibility and accountability for individual nursing judgments and actions.
5. The nurse maintains competence in nursing.
6. The nurse exercises informed judgement and uses individual competence and qualifications as criteria in seeking consultation, accepting responsibilities, and delegating nursing activities to others.
7. The nurse participates in activities that contribute to the ongoing development of the profession's body of knowledge.
8. The nurse participates in the professon's effort to implement and improve standards of nursing.

controlling agencies – Kontrollbehörden, **subsequently** – folglich, **to refine** – verfeinern, **in the interest** – im Interesse, **to examplify** – verdeutlichen, **in accordance** – im Einklang, **abbreviated** – gekürzt, **to provide services** – verfügbar machen von Diensten, **uniqueness** – Einmaligkeit, **unrestricted** – ungemindert, **to safeguard** – beschützen, **judiciously** – wachsam, **to assume** – übernehmen, **accountability** – Beweisführung, **nursing judgements** – pflegerische Entscheidungen, **informed judgement** – wissensbasierte Entscheidung, **to seek** – suchen, **body of knowledge** – Wissensfundus

9. The nurse participates in the profession's effort to establish and maintain conditions of employment conducive to high quality nursing care.
10. The nurse participates in the professon's effort to protect the public from misinformation and misrepresentation, and to maintain the integrity of nursing.
11. The nurse collaborates with members of the health professions and other citizens in promoting community and national efforts to meet the health needs of the public (Kay Kittrell Chitty, 1997).

Professional Ethics are taught in nursing education and different aspects of it are delt with in daily practice. Having background knowledge as well as practical experience about ethical issues of their profession enables nurses to effectively deal with ethical questions in the nursing field. Furthermore, it enables them to be capable participants in the Medical Ethics Commission/Medical Moral Committee (see chapter 3, Medical Ethics Commission).

4.7 Nursing Personnel

The department of Nursing employs different categories of nursing personnel (see this chapter, Organization Chart Nursing Department). Following, some categories/positions are selected and their **main duties** described.

4.7.1 Quality Assurance Coordinator

This person is a registered nurse. She develops certain quality standards for the nursing department as well as interdisciplinary standards and ensures their implementation. She teaches nurses and other hospital staff in matters related to quality. She heads quality circles. She keeps statistics as to quality outcomes and submits these to the director of nursing and hospital administration.

4.7.2 DRG Coordinator

This person is a registered nurse. She checks the record of every new admission regarding the principal diagnosis as well as additional diagnoses. She confers with physicians to ascertain that all possible diagnoses have been listed. She works with nurses on the different nursing floors* to ensure that the allowed length of stay of individual patients is not exceeded. She teaches nurses about the DRG system. She keeps statistics on the course of this system for different diagnostic groups. She negotiates with insurance companies about patients' stay.

* The nursing floor, the nursing unit, the ward = die Pflegestation. The nursing station = das Stationszimmer.

conducive – fördernd, **to meet** – erfüllen, **background knowledge** – Hintergrundwissen, **ethical issues** – ethische Aspekte, **to deal with** – behandeln, **capable** – fähig, **main duties** – Hauptaufgaben, **matters** – Angelegenheiten, **to head** – leiten, **regarding** – hinsichtlich, **to confer** – besprechen, **to ascertain** – sicherstellen, **length of stay** – Verweildauer, **exceeded** – überzogen, **course** – Verlauf, **to negotiate** – verhandeln

4.7.3 Nursing Supervisor

This person is a registered nurse. A Nursing Supervisor is a line manager. There are Nursing Supervisors present on all three shifts. Due to their 24 hour presence they effectively support nurses in their work on the different floors and thus add to the quality of patient care.
By making frequent rounds the supervisor is aware of the amount and intensity of work on the nursing floors and can send additional personnel, arrange for patient transfers, assist in crises situations (i.e. resuscitation), take care of relatives, confer with physicians.

The Nursing Supervisors on the evening and night shift, in addition to their nursing service responsibilities, take care of and are in charge of all departments of the hospital in the absence of their department heads. (For detailed information on the Nursing Supervisor in German, see: *Kellnhauser* 1990.)

4.7.4 Head Nurse

A Head Nurse, also called patient care coordinator is a registered nurse and has similar responsibilities as a head nurse has in Germany. In addition to her leading, organizing and teaching responsibilities she has to keep statistics in such areas as infection control, quality assurance, patient satisfaction, DRG development. She designs the annual budget for her nursing unit, works with and controls her budget. She submits statistics about the economic situation in her area to the director of nursing.

4.7.5 Staff Nurse

A staff nurse is a registered nurse with much the same responsibilities of a staff nurse in Germany. Her basic work structure is the nursing process. She instructs, supports and supervises Licensed Practical Nurses, Nursing Assistants,and other non-professional personnel.

4.7.6 Charge Nurse

To be in charge means to be authorized and responsible. A Charge Nurse is a registered nurse authorized to make nursing decisions and is made responsible for everything that happens on the nursing floor in the absence of the head nurse. Most times she is the assistant head nurse. But any registered nurse can be designated Charge Nurse for one shift or longer by the head nurse or the nursing supervisor. Generally, Charge Nurses work the afternoon or night shift.

line manager – Fachvorgesetzte, **shifts** – Arbeitsschichten, **due to** – aufgrund von, **presence** – Anwesenheit, **to add** – beitragen, **frequent rounds** – häufige Rundgänge, **amount and intensity** – Arbeitsanfall- und Intensität, **additional personal** – zusätzliches Personal, **patient transfer** – Verlegung, **resuscitation** – reanimation, **relatives** – Angehörige, **to take care of** – betreuen, **to be in charge** – verantwortlich sein, **absence** – Abwesenheit, **to design** – erstellen, **annual budget** – Jahresbudget, **to supervise** – beaufsichtigen, **nursing supervisor** – Abteilungsleitung, **assistant head nurse** – Stellvertretung der Stationsschwester, **admitting nurse** – Aufnahmeschwester, **nursing unit/nursing floor** – Pflegestation, **to designate** – beauftragen

4.7.7 Admitting Nurse

This person is a registered nurse. The Admitting Nurse contacts the physicians regarding the admission of their patients. Quite often she calls the patients at home to inform them of their admission date. She receives the written orders from the physicians for their patients and passes them on to the nursing unit the patient is going to. Frequently she initiates certain ordered tests to be done directly at the time of the patient's arrival and before his admission to the nursing floor. Considering special wishes or needs of patients, she coordinates which room the patient is admitted to between the admission office and the nurses on the nursing unit. This is to ensure that a patient is compatible with the other patient in the room and that both feel comfortable with each other. She assists in assigning rooms close to the nursing station for very ill patients.

4.7.8 Clinical Nurse Specialist

This person is a registered nurse. The Clinical Nurse Specialist holds a masters degree in nursing (2. Universitätsgrad) qualifiying her to work in certain nursing specialties, i.e. in cardiology, orthopedics, children, gynecology, medical/surgical nursing, public health. The Nurse Specialist has an expanded knowledge in one of the nursing specialties and generally works on the nursing floors teaching and supporting nurses in complex nursing situations. She includes the nurses on the nursing floors in her research projects and thus ensures the transfer of research results into nursing practice.

4.7.9 Licensed Practical Nurse

The Licensed Practical Nurse = LPN, also called the Licensed Vocational Nurse = LVN, has 2 years of nursing education and after passing final examinations receives a professional license. She assists in the assessment, planning, implementation and evaluation of patient care. Her scope of action is limited as laid down in her job description.

4.7.10 Nursing Assistant

The Nursing Assistant = NA has no formal nursing education. Before or at the time of employment the NA attends an out-of-hospital or in-hospital specific training course of several weeks. While employed by the hospital she receives further on-the-job practical as well as theoretical instructions. Her scope of action too is limited as stated in her job description.

Every category of personnel in nursing has a position description which deliniates their scope of work. Every category works within the parameters of their position description. Registered Nurses are careful with the type of work they delegate to lesser qualified persons

admission – Aufnahme, **written orders** – schriftliche Verordnungen, **to pass on** – weiterleiten, **to assist** – mithelfen, **to assign** – zuteilen, **nursing station** – Stationszimmer, **expanded knowledge** – erweitertes Fachwissen, **nursing floors** – Pflegestationen, **to include** – miteinbeziehen, **scope of action** – Aktionsbereich, **to attend** – mitmachen, **position description** – Tätigkeitsbeschreibung, **scope of work** – Arbeitsaufgaben, **to delineate** – festlegen, **within the parameters** – innerhalb der Grenzen

since they are responsible for the execution of this work and can lose their professional licence in case of serious mistakes.

4.7.11 Volunteers

The volunteer system is well established at American hospitals. The volunteer is a welcome helper on the nursing floor. Generally, the head nurse determines the kind of work a volunteer may perform on the nursing unit. Typical activities of such a person are: Dispense news papers, bring mail, read to patients, bring library books and return them, shop for patients, make phone calls for the patients, help with passing food trays.
A written statement exists about the kind of work a volunteer can do and can not do. This statement is handed to every volunteer upon their starting to work at the hospital.

4.8 Inservice Education

Inservice Education is part of every nursing service department in American hospitals. Following, the objective of such a department and its main areas of work are described.

Objective
The overall objective of the hospital based Inservice Education Department is employee development, especially nursing staff development.

Teaching Personnel
The nurse teachers in this department hold a bachelor or masters degree in nursing. The director of the department usually holds a masters degree in nursing and education.

Main Areas of Work
The work of the Inservice Education Department focuses on four main areas:
Orientation – Staff Needs – Required Education – Patient Education.

4.8.1 Orientation

Employee Orientation
All new employees are taken through an orientation period. This usually means one or more weeks in the classroom where they receive the Employee Handbook and are familiarized with its content (see chapter 6, Employee handbook). They can ask questions and discuss their concerns with the classroom teacher. Also during this time they are given a walking tour through the hospital to learn about the location of different departments. After the completion of this orientation time the individuals start to work in their respective depart-

execution – Ausführung, **serious** – ernsthaft, **volunteer system** – freiwillige Helfer-System, **to determine** – bestimmen, **is handed to** – wird ausgegeben, **inservice education** – Innerbetriebliche Fortbildung, **educational needs** – Bildungsbedürfnisse, **masters degree in education** – Mastergrad in Pflege und Erziehungswissenschaften, **orientation** – Einführung, **employees** – Mitarbeiter, **orientation period** – Einführungszeit, **to familiarize** – bekanntmachen

ments. Periodically thereafter they receive instructions about new developments in their specific areas of work, i.e. the utilization of new machines or the implementation of new saftey regulations.

Nursing Staff Orientation

Although the inservice teachers are responsible for satisfying the educational needs of all employees their special focus is on nursing education. Consequently, each category of newly employed nursing personnel is taken through an orientation period in the classroom. Like all other employees they are given the basic rules and regulations about employment (see chapter 6, Employee Handbook). They are also tested about their level of professional knowledge and capability. Class room instruction for registered nurses usually last 4 weeks or longer depending on their overall proficiency (see chapter 6, Nursing Orientation).

The orientation on the nursing floor or in a nursing specialty area is usually done by assigning a preceptor, which is an experienced nurse to the newly employed nurse for a period of 2–4 months. This means that they both work the same shifts until the newcomer feels secure in her work performance. Frequent criteria based performance evaluations are conducted by the head nurse with the new employee in order to document progress and to provide help where needed.

4.8.2 Nursing Staff Needs

Educational needs of the nursing staff are found out in two ways. One methode is to let the staff members name certain work related educational topics. This is done informally by nurses talking to teachers of the inservice education department. Or it is done formally by the department distributing questionnaires to the nursing staff asking for their input. In both cases the appropriate classes are set up.

The second method to find out about educational needs is by direct observation of individual nurses during their work performance. Head nurses, nursing colleagues or nursing supervisors suggest, where necessary, to the particular nurse her need of education on specific matters. The inservice department takes care of the individual's need.

In some cases the need on specific educational points may be determined during the time of the annual individual job performance evaluation (see chapter 6, Performance Evaluation). These specific individual deficits can be eliminated with the help of the inservice education department.

utilization – Nutzung, **to satisfy** – befriedigen, **educational needs** – Bildungsbedürfnisse, **nursing education** – pflegerische Bildung, **nursing personnel** – Pflegepersonal, **overall proficiency** – Gesamtfähigkeiten, **specialty area** – Funktionsbereich, **secure** – sicher, **work performance** – Arbeitsleistung, **performance evaluations** – Arbeitsbewertung, **nursing staff** – Pflegepersonal, **work related** – arbeitsbezogen, **topics** – Themen, **inservice education department** – Innerbetriebliche Fortbildungsabteilung, **questionnaires** – Fragebogen, **to suggest** – vorschlagen, **specific matters** – bestimmte Punkte, **job performance evaluation** – Arbeitsleistungsbewertung, **to eliminate** – beheben

Occasionally qualitiy management statistics show the need for nursing education, i.e. in the case of a certain increase in medication errors, or an increase in infection incidents. In such instances either individual or group instruction classes are set up.

At times new and hitherto unknown diseases occur, as was the case with AIDS. This means that in cases like this, the inservice department has to educate not only the complete nursing staff but also all other hospital employees in this matter.

4.8.3 Required Education

The external control agencies require several different types of ongoing education. One example of the kind of ongoing education demanded is the Joint Commission's requirement (see chapter 3, A Quality Controlling Agency) that all hospital personnel dealing with patients has to be proficient in the performance of patient resuscitation. At inspection time the departments have to show proof that their personnel has annually attended and successfully passed the practice sessions on resuscitation.Therefore the inservice education department has to schedule and conduct these educational sessions for the appropriate personnel.

Another example is the State controlling agencies requirement that hospital personnel act effectively in times of emergencies such as fire, bomb threats or an unusual influx of emergency patients. Consequently, the inservice department sets up the annually/semi-annually required drills, monitors and documents the results, especially the deficits of the performance, and sets up classes to eliminate them.

These few examples of the work of the inservice education department are simply an excerpt of the wide spectrum of the department's educational activities. Still, the department can not cover all educational topics in nursing. Therefore, nurses are sent to appropriate educational conferences, seminars or workshops outside the hospital. The time spent in education is considered work time. The expenses are paid by the hospital out of a special education budget. Employees attending academic study courses and having to pay tuition can expect financial help from the hospital. This is especially helpful for nurses who work part time and study full time.
The prevailing idea in American hopitals about the education of all employees is: The more our personnel is educated the more our human resource potential is increased and the better we are fortified to win in the competitive health care market (see chapter 6, Benefits).

medication errors – Fehler bei Arzneimittelvergabe, **incident** – Vorkommnis, **hitherto** – bislang, **to occur** – erscheinen, **ongoing** – fortlaufend, **proficient** – fähig, **resuscitation** – Reanimation, **to show proof** – belegen, **to schedule** – terminieren, **to conduct** – durchführen, **state controlling agencies** – staatliche Kontrollbehörden, **bomb threats** – Bombendrohungen, **drills** – Übungen, **tuition** – Studiengebühren, **prevailing idea** – vorherrschende Meinung, **the more** – je mehr, **to be fortified** – gestärkt sein, **competitive** – wettbewerblich

4.8.4 Patient Education

Within the Inservice Education Department there is usually one sub-department responsible for patient education. Depending on the size of the hospital one or more nurse educators work on patient education. They create booklets, films or other materials on topics like: Cancer and how to avoid it, Dietary Management of Fat and Cholesterol, Mangement of Diabetes (see chapter 3, Television Booklet). The nurse educators are asked by the floor nurses to talk to certain patients about their special educational needs. Subsequently, the patient education nurse conducts one or more sessions with the patient on his particular needs, leaves appropriate information booklets with him, and/or recommends the viewing of special health films on the in-house educational channel.
Nurse educators also teach groups of patients or clients on a variety of topics in health care. The educational interaction between the patient education nurse and the patient facilitates and supports the work of the nurse who is responsible for the total care of the patient.

floor nurses – Krankenschwestern auf Station, **conduct** – durchführen, **variety** – Vielfalt, **to facilitate** – erleichtern, **to support** – unterstützen

5 The Nursing Unit

In diesem Kapitel wird die Pflege von Patienten auf einer Pflegestation aufgezeigt. Dabei wird unterschieden zwischen den hierfür bestehenden strukturellen und methodischen Gegebenheiten. Bei den strukturellen Gegebenheiten wird auf räumliche, personelle und arbeitsmaterielle Aspekte eingegangen. Bei den methodischen Gegebenheiten werden die Rahmenvorgaben erläutert, die beim Ablauf der Betreuung von Patienten zum Tragen kommen.

5.1 Structural Framework for Nursing Care

All nursing units have a certain structural framework within which nursing care is delivered. Patients are nursed on a nursing unit, or a nursing floor, or a ward. These three terms are used for what in German is called »die Station.« **Note: The German term Station – in the sense of an area where patients are nursed – does not exist.** Therefore, using the term »Station« and meaning a patient area will be misunderstood.
The term **Nursing Station** means »das Stationszimmer«. This is a room or most likely an open area which fulfills much the same function as it does in Germany.

5.1.1 The Nursing Station

In the nursing station several books are kept containing helpful information for the daily work of nursing personnel, such as:
The Policy and Procedure Handbooks (see Chapter 4, Policy and Procedure Manuals),
The Quality Assurance Manual,
The Infection Control Manual,
The Disaster/Emergency Manual,
The Red List/Drug Handbook,
The Employee Handbook (see Chapter 6, Employee Handbook),
Several Nursing Journals,
Books about Nursing,
Medical and Nursing Dictionaries.
In many hospitals several of the Handbooks and Manuals are computerized.

The nursing station is largely the domain of the Unit Secretary. Unit Secretaries are present during the morning and the afternoon shifts, which is the time from 7 a.m. until 11.30 p.m, 7 days a week. Her various activities free nurses for their work with patients. Since she interacts with all in-house departments as well as outside agencies and the public at large she is an important representative of the hospital. To ensure that unit secretaries convey a positive

patient area – Patientenbereich, **to contain** – enthalten, **disaster** – Katastrophe, **drug** – Medikament, **to be present** – anwesend sein, **the public at large** – Öffentlichkeit, **to convey** – vermitteln

image of the nursing unit and the hospital in general, most hospitals offer special courses in »the courteous usage of the telephone.« New secretary employees must attend this course and receive a hand book on this topic for further use. (Telephone Communication Skills 1995, Alexian Brothers Medical Center, Chicago; For a job description of a Unit Secretary in German see Kellnhauser 1991.)

Nurses use the nursing station to read in the patients' charts and to do their charting. In the nursing station they speak with their co-workers, physicians, other health care professionals and relatives. Here they use the phone to take doctors' orders and speak with various other hospital departments i.e. X-Ray, Dietary, Laboratory.

Note: *The chart* is the patient record.
***To chart* means to document in the patient record.**

5.1.2 Nursing Personnel

Personnel typically found on a nursing unit are the Head Nurse, Staff Nurses*, LPNs, Nursing Assistants and Unit Secretaries, and possibly Clinical Nurse Specialists. For the main duties of these persons and some other nursing personnel (see Chapter 4, Nursing Personnel).

Another type of RN – Registered Nurse on the nursing unit is the **Private Duty Nurse.** This nurse is not employed by the hospital but by a private nurses agency. The agency is contaced by the department of nursing when a patient wishes to have a private nurse for one or more shifts. The private duty nurse takes care only of this one patient and is fully responsible for all her actions. However, the overall responsibility about the patient remains with the head nurse or charge nurse. Payment for nursing care is forwarded directly to the private duty nurse by the patient or his relatives. Tax and insurances are paid by the nurse. The agency collects a small fee for procuring the job.

There can also be the so called **Agency Nurses.** This RN too is not employed by the hospital and comes from a nurses agency. The agency is contacted by the department of nursing when there is a need for additional nurses on one or more nursing floors. The period of work may be only one shift or several shifts during a week or month. The RN works with the regular nurses on the nursing unit as assigned by the head nurse. She is fully responsible for the patients she is assigned to. However, here too the overall responsibility for the patients remains with the head nurse or charge nurse. Payment for her work is made by the hospital to the agency which in turn pays the nurse. Tax and Insurances are paid either by the nurse or the agency.

* Staff Nurses sind RNs = Registered Nurses

image – Eindruck, **courteous usage** – höfliche Bedienung, **nursing station** – Stationszimmer/Pflegestützpunkt, **chart = patient record** – Krankenakte, **relatives** – Angehörige, **X-Ray** – Röntgenabteilung, **nursing unit** – Station, **overall responsibility** – Gesamtverantwortung, **charge nurse** – stellvertretende Stationsschwester, **tax** – Steuer, **insurances** – Versicherungen, **to procure** – beschaffen, **to assign** – festlegen, **in turn** – ihrerseits

Quite often the **Home Health Care Nurse** comes from her agency to the nursing floor to check on patients who are soon to be discharged and transferred to home health care. She speaks with the patient and with the RN taking care of the patient. She also checks the patient's chart to gather information in order to arrange for the continuation of appropriate nursing care after discharge.

Another person on the nursing unit is the **Respiratory Therapist**. This specialist has a university education in pulmonology and takes care of patients in need of various pulmonary treatments on the nursing floors and the intensive care units as ordered by the physician.On the nursing floors these treatments are usually different types of inhalations, pre- and post-operative breathing exercises. He maintaines the proper functioning of all respirators on the nursing floors and the intensive care units and works closely with the RNs in all aspects of this special kind of patient care. Respiratory Therapists usually work on all three shifts 7 days a week.

5.1.3 Work Uniforms

The different categories of nursing personnel can usually be differentiated by the type of uniform they wear. There is a written uniform code according to which RNs and LPNs wear white uniforms. Nursing Assistants have some color accent to their uniforms. In recent years many hospitals have made concessions to the observance of the uniform code (see Buckley-Viertel, 2001) while others still strictly adhere to it.The unit secretaries wear a business like attire. The uniforms have to be bought and maintained by the employees.

Name Tags have to be worn by all employees at all times. A typical Name Tag of an RN may read: Betty Miller, RN, BSN, Department of Nursing (see Fig. 5). This Name Tag shows that this person is a Registered Nurse and that she holds an academic degree, the BSN, which is the Bachelor of Science in Nursing (see chapter 7, Ways of Nursing Education). And that she works in the Department of Nursing. Another Name Tag may read: Anne Smith, NA, Departement of Nursing. This name tag shows that the person is a nursing assistant in the Department of Nursing. Since patients clearly know the educational difference between a registered nurse, a nursing assistant and other nursing personnel it is important that the Name Tags give the qualifications of the persons the patient is dealing with. Name Tags also show relatives, visitors and physicians the professional qualification of the nursing person they are speaking to. This is especially important for physicians since they can only give medical orders to an RN.

to discharge – entlassen, **to transfer** – verlegen, **chart** – Patientenakte, **appropriate care** – entsprechende Pflege, **ordered** – verordnet, **respirators** – Beatmungsapparate, **work uniforms** – Arbeitskleidung, **to differentiate** – unterscheiden, **uniform code** – Arbeitskleidungsvorschrift, **LPNs = Licenced Practical Nurses** – Schesternhelferinnen, **nursing assistants** – ungelernte Helferinnen, **concessions** – Zugeständnisse, **observance** – Einhaltung, **to adhere** – festhalten, **attire** – Bekleidung, **to maintain** – erhalten, **name tag** – Namensschild, **medical orders** – Verordnungen

Fig. 5: Name tag.

Fig. 6: School pin.

Increasingly the Name Tag is being replaced with the identification badge. The I.D. badge shows the same information as the name tag plus a photo of the wearer.

RNs and LPNs wear their nursing school pins to demonstrate their affection for their place of education (see Fig. 6).

5.1.4 Work Time

The time schedule, also called the work schedule is made out by the head nurse usually 6 weeks in advance and placed on the bulletin board for everyone to see. Wishes regarding special days off are submitted to the head nurse prior to her designing the work schedule.

identification badge – Identifikationskarte, **nursing school pins** – Schulbrosche, **affection** – Verbundenheit, **time schedule** – Dienstplan, **in advance** – im vorhinein, **bulletin board** – Informationsbrett, **days off** – freie Tage, **prior to** – bevor

Full time nursing personnel like all other full time employees works a 40 hour week. This means that a nurse works 8 hours a day and 5 days per week. She has 2 days off per week. The classical shift times are:

7.00 a.m. to 3.30 p.m.
3.00 p.m. to 11.30 p.m.
11.00 p.m. to 7.30 a.m.

The 30 minutes overlap between shifts is used for the nursing report. Nursing report is given either in the nursing station or at the bedside.
During each shift a 15–20 minute break and a 30 minute meal break are given.

Most hospitals have the system of nursing personnel working rotating shifts. But there are also those where nursing personnel works their chosen shift without rotating.
Some nursing units work – at the request of the nurses – 12 hour shifts. These run generally from 7 a.m.–7 p.m. and from 7 p.m.–7 a.m. The same regulation regarding breaks applies as stated above.
Besides different shifts for full time nursing employees, several models of part time work exist.

5.1.5 Nursing Systems

The team nursing system is widely practised. At the beginning of each shift the head nurse or charge nurse assign nursing personnel to certain teams. Care is taken that the members of a team remain the same as much as possible in order to provide continuation of care.

Primary nursing is utilized in hospitals on certain nursing floors or special units. Generally, the patients admitted to the primary care units have multiple nursing care needs and require intense nursing.

Functional nursing is also practiced in certain areas. The utilization of this nursing system usually increases in times of nursing shortages.

In all three systems the head nurse or charge nurse makes the assignment of nurses to patients at the beginning of each shift and determines break times for each person during the shift.Care is taken that the assignments maintain continuity of care. In order to guard patient safety a minimal number of personnel is off the floor for breaks at any given time.

overlap – Überschneidung, **meal** – Essen, **break** – pause, **rotating shifts** – Schichtdienst, **request** – Anfrage/Wunsch, **regulation** – Vorschrift, **to assign** – zuteilen, **to remain** – verbleiben, **nursing shortage** – Schwesternmangel, **assignment** – Zuteilung, **off the floor** – weg von der Station

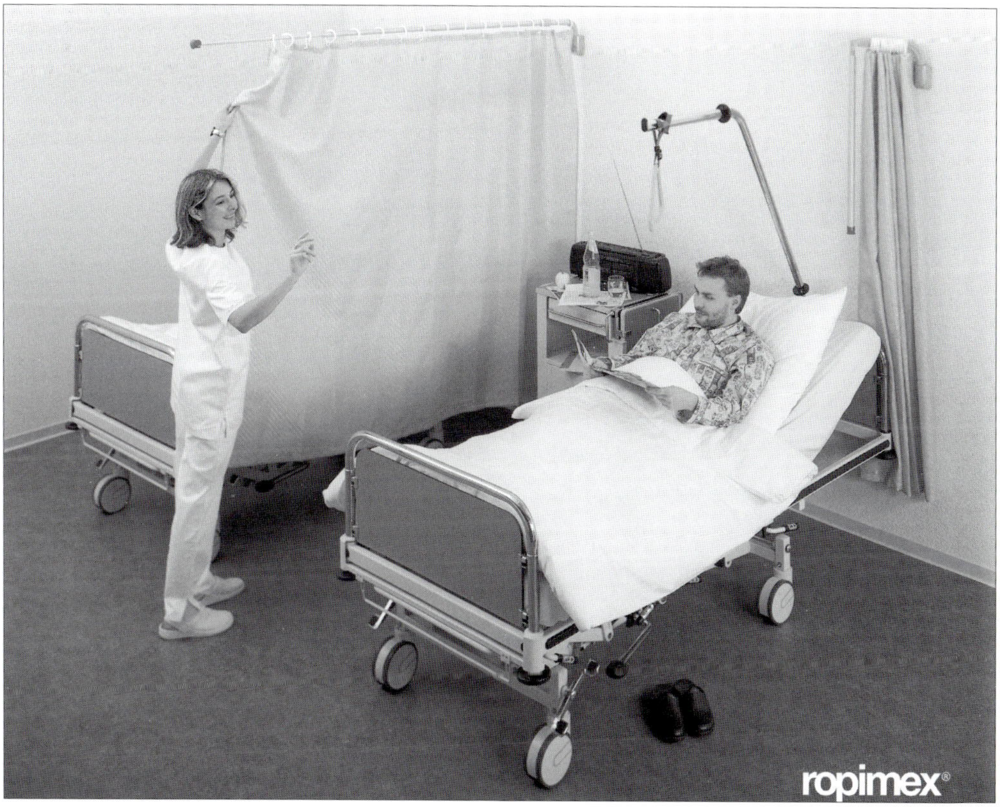

Fig. 7: Ropimex

5.1.6 Patients' Rooms

The majority of hospitals has so called semi-private rooms. This means that there are 2 beds to each patient room. Each room has a bathroom with wash basin, toilet and shower. Frequently the patients' rooms and the corridors are carpeted. Each room has a television set and each patient has a telephone free of charge for local calls. Usually there are wall outlets for oxygen and suction. Attached to the ceiling are washable curtains which are drawn around the bed each time nursing staff or physicians give certain care or treatments to the patient (see Fig. 7). Standard equipment in all patient rooms is an electric bed which enables the patient to change the position of the head and foot part. It also enables the nursing staff to place the bed in high/low position. In especially well equipped hospitals the bed can be put in Trendelenburg/Shock position by using a foot pedal at the end of the bed. All beds have adjustable side rails. The color of the beds, the night stands and the bed tables are of

to guard – darüber wachen, **carpet** – Teppich, **free of charge** – kostenlos, **wall outlets** – Wandanschlüsse, **suction** – Saugung, **to attach** – anbringen, **ceiling** – Zimmerdecke, **curtain** – Vorhang, **to equip** – ausstatten, **adjustable side rails** – anpassungsfähiges Bettgitter, **night stand** – Nachtkästchen

brown, wooden or wood like material. Light colored drapes and suitable pictures complete the furnishings of the room. The idea is to get away from the white, cold environment of a hospital and to create a home like atmosphere.

5.1.7 Transporting Patients

Patients having to leave the nursing unit for any reason, i.e. to have an X-Ray, an EKG, or certain laboratory tests done, are taken to the special departments by wheel chair by a member of the transportation department. This is a precautionary measure intended to provide safety for the patient and to prevent accidents. Subsequently, the hospital keeps insurance claims low and thereby prevents an increase in insurance premiums.

5.2 Methods in Nursing Care

In caring for patients nurses perform countless different nursing tasks utilizing certain methods. Of these numerous nursing tasks specific ones are selected and the methods used in carrying them out are described.

5.2.1 Admitting Patients

Having gone through the admission office the patient is brought to the nursing floor in a wheel chair by a member of the transportation department (see this chapter, Transporting Patients). He is greeted by the unit secretary and the nurses who happen to be in the nursing station. His admission papers are taken and his identification bracelet (see I.D. Bracelet Chapter 3, The Patient) is checked by the RN assigned to him. This nurse will familiarize the patient with his room, introduce him to his fellow patient and explain the functioning of the equipment in the room. She will then initiate the nursing process by conducting the admission interview. Discharge* planning starts at admission. Therefore, it is important that the RN speaks with the patient and accompanying relatives about his health care situation after discharge from the hospital.

* Discharge = Entlassung eines Patienten, Discharge from a wound = Wundsekret

drapes – Vorhänge, **furnishings** – Mobiliar, **X-Ray** – Röntgenaufnahme, **wheel chair** – Rollstuhl, **precautionary measure** – Vorsichtsmaßnahme, **accidents** – Unfälle, **insurance claims** – Versicherungsansprüche, **nursing tasks** – pflegerische Tätigkeiten, **to select** – auswählen, **to carry out** – durchführen, **to describe** – beschreiben, **admission office** – Aufnahmebüro, **familiarize** – bekannt machen, **to introduce** – vorstellen, **fellow patient** – Mitpatient, **equipment** – Ausstattung, **relatives** – Angehörige

Physician's Orders

Diagnoses: ______________________________

1. o.o. bed ad lib = out of bed ad lib
   Darf uneingeschränkt aufstehen

2. Salt free diet
   Salzlose Kost

3. I+O = Intake and Output
   Flüssigkeitsbilanz

4. Fluid Restriction 1500 cc/24 h
   Flüssigkeitszufuhr eingeschränkt 1500 cc/24 Stunden

5. O2 2 l /min. nasal cannula
   Sauerstoff 2 l /Minute per Sauerstoffsonde

6. Weigh q.o.d.
   Wiegen jeden 2. Tag

7. CBC = Complete Blood Count
   Großes Blutbild

8. Lytes = Electrolytes
   Electrolyte, E'lytes

9. EKG
   EKG

10. Mylanta 30 cc po q.i.d. and prn
    Mylanta 30 cc per os 4x täglich und bei Bedarf

11. Digoxin 0.25 mg po q.d.
    Digoxin 0.25 mg per os täglich

12. Lasix 40 mg i.m. stat and b.i.d.
    Lasix 40 mg i.m. sofort und 2x täglich

13. Valium 5 mg po hs
    Valium 5 mg per os zur Nacht

14. Demerol 50 mg i.m. q 4 h prn
    Demerol 50 mg i.m. bei Bedarf alle 4 Stunden

Phone orders 2.10 pm Dr. Brown, B. Smith, RN

Fig. 8: Physician's Order sheet.

5.2.2 Physician's Orders

When a patient is admitted medical orders have to be obtained for him from his attending physician. There are different ways to obtain physician's orders.
One way is, upon the patient's admission to the nursing unit the unit secretary or the RN assigned to the patient calls the patient's attending physician to inform him of the admission. At this time the physician will give his medical orders to the RN via telephone. Only the RN, on account of her qualification and responsibility, is allowed by hospital policy to take orders from a physician via phone. She writes the orders on the physician's order sheet and notes »phone orders«, date and time, the physician's name, her name and professional qualification. The physician is aware that hospital regulations require that these orders have to be signed by him within 24 hours and will do so. Verbal orders given by the physician to the nurse during the time of the patient's stay have to be written on the order sheet by the nurse and signed by the physician. During his regular visits with the patient the physician will write his new or changed orders in the physician's order sheet.

Fig. 8 shows a physician's order sheet with typical medical orders. The orders displayed here are not based on any diagnoses. The purpose of presenting this example is simply to show how orders are given and how some of the common abbreviations are used (see list of abbreviations in Appendix). To facilitate understanding, each line of the orders in English is translated into German.

Since there is a nursing standard for taking vital signs: Temperature, Pulse and Respiration = TPR and Blood Pressure = BP on all newly admitted patients the physician does not order this nursing task.

Another way to obtain physician's orders from the attending physician for his patient admitted to the hospital is by entering orders directly into the computer on the nursing unit from hand held palm devices or via a computer system in the doctor's office.

Still another way for the same purpose is to use the telephone sytems to dial into the computer on the nursing unit. An electronic signature appears on the paper copy.

Aside from Physician's orders there are also nursing orders, i.e. if an RN assesses a patient in danger of developing a bed sore she can order and use appropriate skin protective material for him.The nursing orders have to be verified by signature of the attending physician for the purpose of insurance payment.

orders – Verordnungen, **attending physician** – behandelnder Arzt, **admission** – Aufnahme, **hopital policy** – Krankenhausrichtlinien, **physician's order sheet** – ärztliches Verordnungsformular, **to sign** – unterschreiben, **common abbreviations** – gewöhnlich angewandte Abkürzungen, **nursing task** – pflegerische Aufgabe, **devices** – Geräte, **doctor's office** – ärztliche Praxis, **to appear** – erscheinen, **danger** – Gefahr, **bed sore** – Dekubitus, **protection** – Schutz, **to verify** – beglaubigen, **insurance** – Versicherung

5.2.3 Physician's Progress Notes

No matter how often a physician visits a patient during the day, he will each time write a progress note stating the patient's current medical condition, his plan of treatment and frequently the expected outcome. All members of the therapeutic team and especially nurses have access to the progress notes (see this chapter, The Chart) and can orient their care on the current medical plan. This is especially helpful for part time nurses, nurses back from days off or from vacation (see this chapter, Nursing Personnel) as well as other personnel who do not take care of the patient in a continuous manner. Simply by reading the physician's progress notes as well as the nurses notes and care plan they have a good overall picture about the current condition of the patient.

5.2.4 Medications

Medications are given to patients by RNs or LPNs according to physician's orders. The times of the medications ordered are strictly adhered to. i.e. If a drug is ordered q.i.d. (see Physician's Order Sheet, Fig. 8) it is given at 10 a.m.–2 p.m.–6 p.m.– and 10 p.m. (other times see appendix, Abbreviations). This system of using certain standard times for giving medications is practised in all American hospitals.

5.2.5 The Chart

The Chart contains the complete information/documentation about the patient. This means all documents regarding the patient, i.e. medical examinations, laboratory results, X-Ray reports, surgery reports, doctors' orders, medical progress notes, dietary plans, nursing notes, reports of various other health specialists are placed in this ring binder (see Fig. 9).

The chart is kept in the nursing station. It is available to all disciplines involved in the care and treatment of the patient. The chart has color coded divisions labelled as follows (see Fig. 10):

Physician Orders
The form for medical orders is placed here (see exhibit Nr. 8., this chapter).

Medical Staff Records
The forms for documentation of the medical history and physical examination, and the notes about the progress of the patient are placed here.

Cardiovascular/EEG Pulmonary Reports
Results of tests in these specialties are placed here.

physician's progress notes – Ärztliche Dokumentation des Krankheitsverlaufs, **current** – aktuell, **plan of treatment** – Behandlungsplan, **part time** – Teilzeit, **vacation** – Urlaub, **nurses notes** – Pflegedokumentation, **overall picture** – Gesamtbild, **to adhere** – einhalten/festhalten, **chart** – Patientenakte, **X-Ray** – Röntgenberichte, **medical progress notes** – Behandlungsergebnisse-/pläne, **nursing notes** – Pflegebericht, **to be involved** – befasst sein, **to label** – beschriften, **medical staff-records** – ärztliche Dokumentation, **medical history** – Krankheitsgeschichte

Fig. 9: The Chart, closed; Zeichnung Rudolf Wachter.

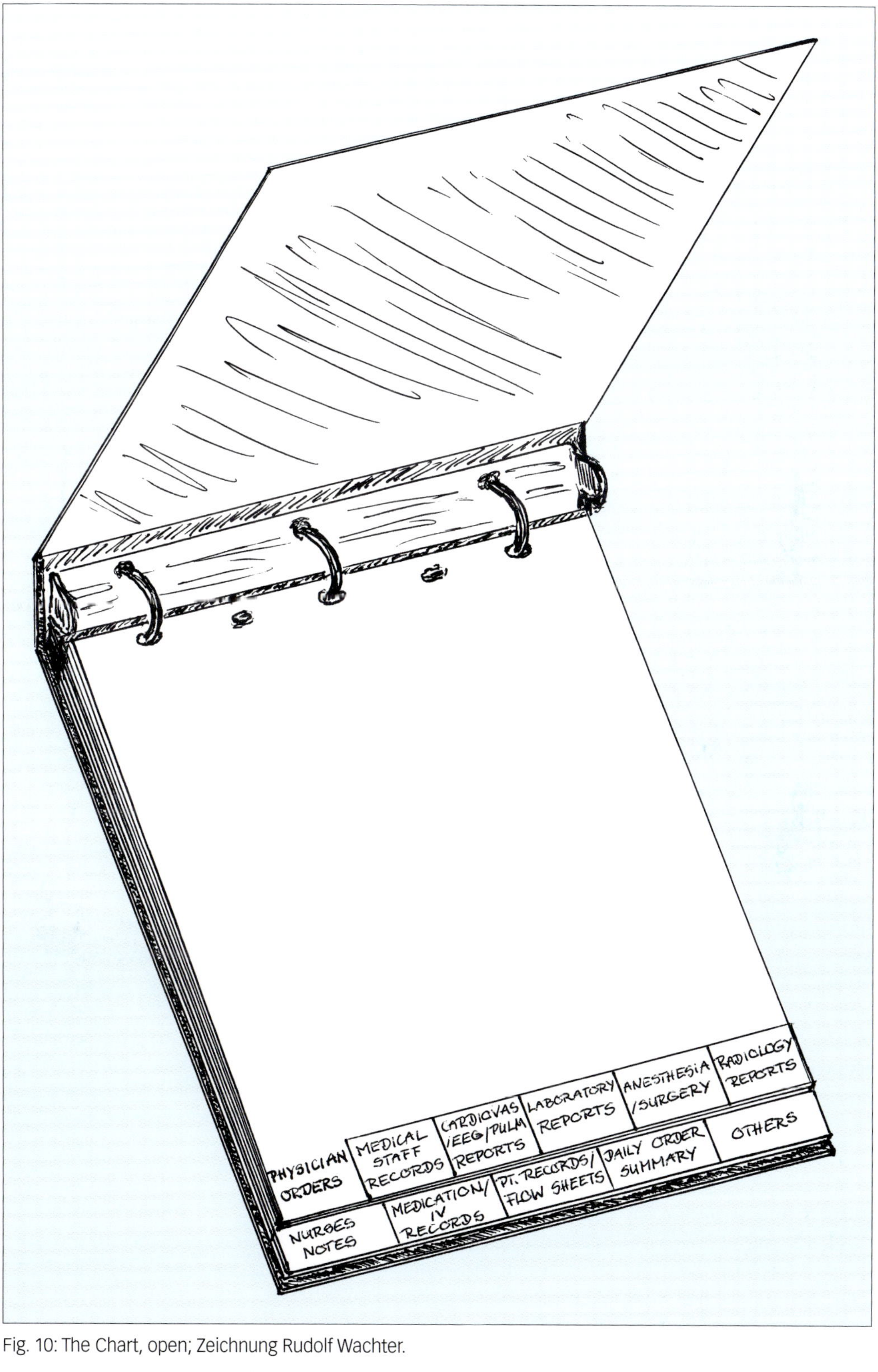

Fig. 10: The Chart, open; Zeichnung Rudolf Wachter.

Laboratory Reports
Results of laboratory tests go here.

Anethesia/Surgery
Reports of treatments in these specialties go here.

Radiology Reports
Dokumentation of services provided by the X-Ray department is placed here.

Nurses Notes
Documentation of all nursing care services is placed here.

Medication/IV Records
Documentation of medications given including intravenous treatment is placed here.

Patient Records/Flow Sheets
Nursing documentation of special care of the patient as well as flow sheets, i.e. Neurological Checks, Intake and Output, Diabetic Record, Frequent Blood Pressure checks are placed here.

Daily Order Summary
Computer print outs giving an overview of a 24 hour order profile go here.

Others
Documentation of services provided by departments like the dietary, social work, physiotherapy, pastoral care, and others goes here.

5.2.6 Nursing Documentation

As far as nursing is concerned, all documentation of nursing care, except flow sheets and medication records is placed under the division *Nurses Notes*. On the first form in this division the general *Admission Information* is documented. On the following four pages a detailed *Admission Patient Profile* is established which is the basis for determining the various nursing diagnoses and the designing of the nursing care plan. The form for discharge planning is placed here. Following are pages called *Patient Progress Notes*. On these pages nursing care, the response of the patient to the care, and the condition of the patient from a nursing point of view is charted by each shift. Charting has to be done in such a way that any person can follow the patient's progress or regress during the whole time of his hospital stay. All documentation is to be signed by family name and qualification of the nursing person giving the care.
An *Interdisciplinary Communication/Conference Form* is for the documentation of interdisciplinary patient conferences (see chapter 4, Policy and Procedure).

intake and output – Flüssigkeitsbilanz, **blood pressure** – Blutdruck, **order summary** – Verordnungsübersicht, **division** – Abschnitt, **admission** – Aufnahme, **to determine** – festlegen, **discharge planing** – Entlassungsplanung, **to chart** – dokumentieren, **progress or regress** – Besserung oder Verschlechterung, **hospital stay** – Krankenhausaufenthalt, **to sign** – unterschreiben

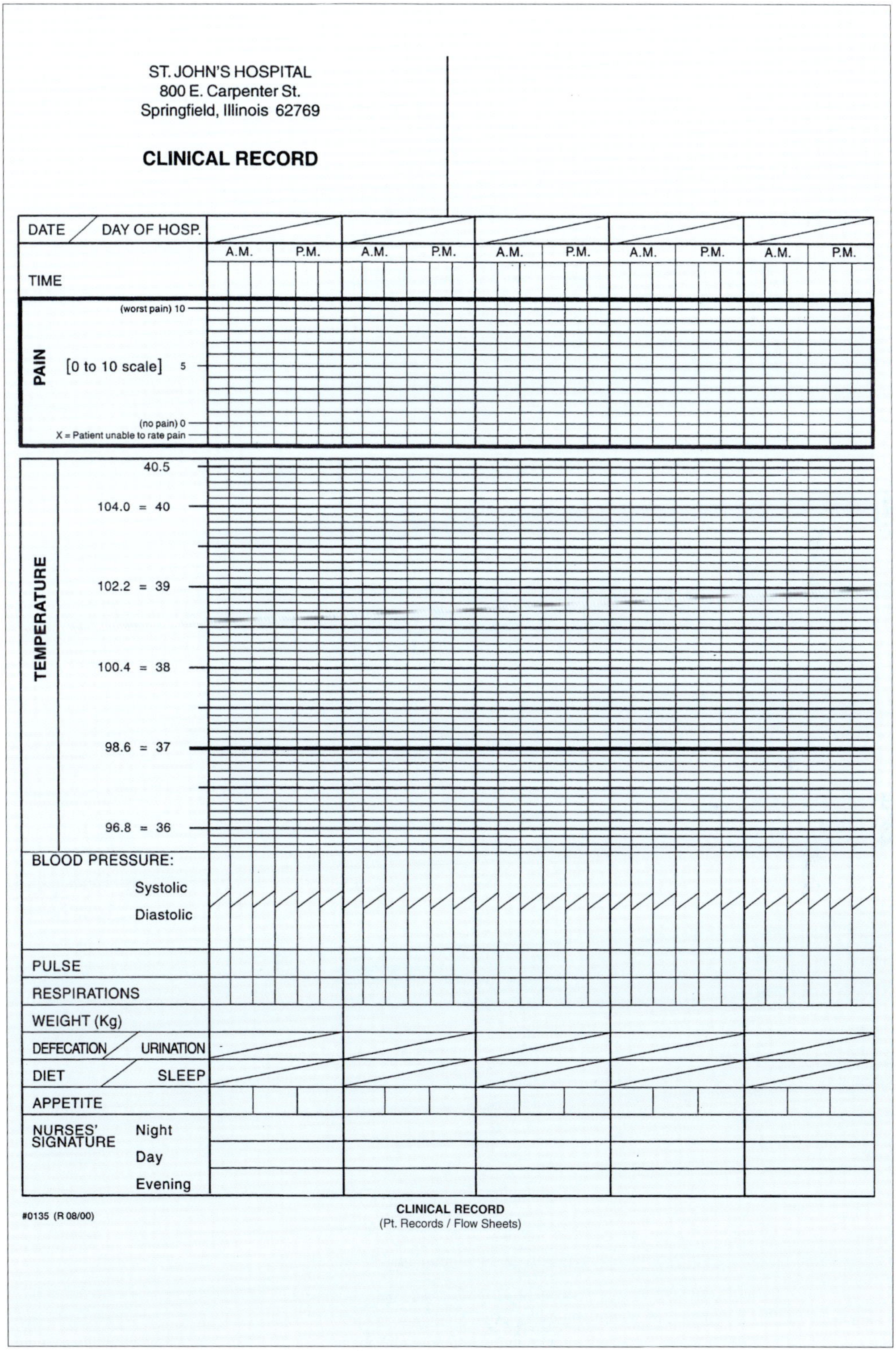
ST. JOHN'S HOSPITAL
800 E. Carpenter St.
Springfield, Illinois 62769

CLINICAL RECORD

DATE / DAY OF HOSP.										
	A.M.	P.M.	A.M.	P.M.	A.M.	P.M.	A.M.	P.M.	A.M.	P.M.
TIME										
PAIN [0 to 10 scale] (worst pain) 10										
5										
(no pain) 0										
X = Patient unable to rate pain										
TEMPERATURE 40.5										
104.0 = 40										
102.2 = 39										
100.4 = 38										
98.6 = 37										
96.8 = 36										
BLOOD PRESSURE: Systolic / Diastolic										
PULSE										
RESPIRATIONS										
WEIGHT (Kg)										
DEFECATION / URINATION										
DIET / SLEEP										
APPETITE										
NURSES' SIGNATURE Night										
Day										
Evening										

#0135 (R 08/00)

CLINICAL RECORD
(Pt. Records / Flow Sheets)

Fig. 11: Clinical record form.

In the *Discharge Forms* the condition of the patient at discharge is documented. These include a copy of the written instructions given to the patient and/or his family to take home.

Nursing flow sheets are placed under the division *Patient Records/Flow Sheets*. In the so called *Clinical Record Form* the following items are charted: the date, the number of days of the patient's stay, and the time. The time is divided in A.M. and P.M. columns. On a pain scale of 1 to 10 the intensity of pain is recorded. The temperature is given in measurements of Fahrenheit and Celsius indicating the normal points by a dark line.
Further documentation pertains to the vital signs, as there are:Blood Pressure, Pulse and Respiration. **Note:** It is standard practice to count and document the respiration of every patient routinely since the respiration is an essential part of the patient's vital signs. Also charted are the Weight, Defecation/Urination, Diet, Sleep and Appetite. This form as all others provides space for nurses' signatures on all three shifts. Nurses' signature means: family name and professional qualification (see Fig. 11).

The division *Medication/i.v. Records* is for the documentation forms of medications and intravenous infusions. Since charting of medications and intravenous fluids is mostly done on the computer, the appropriate computer print out is placed here showing the medications and intravenous infusions given over each 24 hours and compiled over a 7-day period.
Charting the medication(s) given means: The name of the patient is printed on the forms. For each medication the name of the medication, the dosage, the time and the route of administration are documented. Each time the nurse administers the various medications she signs with her surname and qualification. The same applies for the intravenous infusions.
In case a mistake is made by the nurse as to the correct medication, time, dosage, route, or patient, she has to inform the attending physician as well as the head nurse. She has to fill out a so called »Incident Report Form« wherein the reason for the mistake is stated. The form is submitted to the director of nursing for her information. Thereafter the form is sent to the quality assurance office.
The idea behind this is to keep statistics as to the frequency and type of medication errors in order to eliminate them as much as possible. Where indicated, inservice teaching will help the individual nurse to learn how to avoid this kind of mistakes (see chapter 4, Inservice Education, Staff Needs).

Note: The method of charting shown above is the traditional way of documenting nursing care. This method is still used in many hospitals today. However, there are also those where all charting is computerized and no paper print out exists. Currently, most hospitals are somewhere between those two methods. This means, some documenting by hand is done and some computer charting is done and paper copies of the latter are printed out and placed in the chart.

patient's stay – Verweildauer, **to divide** – einteilen, **to pertain** – zugehören, **vital signs** – vitale Zeichen, **to compile** – zusammenfügen, **administration** – Vergabe, **surname** – Familienname, **to apply** – gelten, **mistake** – Fehler, **frequency** – Häufigkeit, **error** – Fehler, **inservice teaching** – innerbetriebliche Fortbildung, **to avoid** – vermeiden

The chart, also called the patient record is identical in appearance in all hospitals of the United States.This means, every hospital uses the same kind of chart. Sometimes the outside cover may be brown instead of blue or green. But the inside divisions are the same. Forms can differ slightly according to individual hospital design.

5.2.7 Evaluating Nursing Care

The evaluation of nursing care is routinely carried out as part of nursing practice. There are different ways to evaluate nursing care.

One way is to do an ongoing evaluation of nursing care on the basis of planned care delivered and the patient's response to it. Depending on this response nursing care is continually adjusted to effect maximal benefit for the patient. This evaluation is carried out by the RNs taking care of the patient while he is in the hospital.

Another way is to evaluate nursing care after the patient is discharged. Using this method RNs review a certain number of patient records with the same diagnosis, i.e. 30 records of patients with the diagnosis diabetes mellitus. Comparing the nursing documentation with the existing detailed criteria for nursing care of patients with this diagnosis, the percentage of the quality of nursing care reached for these 30 patients is determined.

Another method for determining the degree of the quality of nursing care is comparing the nursing documentation of one nursing unit with that of another unit on the same nursing problem. This is done by some RNs of both units. For instance: Nursing unit A compares its nursing documentation about bed sore prevention with the documentation about bed sore prevention with nursing unit B. Both units work with the same standard for bed sore prevention. The results of this comparison usually indicate areas for improvement in one or both of the nursing units. A time period is set by which the agreed upon improvement has to be achieved and a date is fixed for the next review.
Using such procedures for quality control a collegial exchange of ideas takes place about how to further improve nursing care quality. The positive results of this work enhance collegial understanding and cooperation.

Nurses are not only involved in evaluating nursing care but they are members in quality assurance committees checking on the interdisciplinary quality of care. i.e. An interdisciplinary committee for quality of care in the department of orthopedics may consist of: A Physio-Therapist, Orthopedic Surgeon, Nurse, Pharmacist, Blood Bank Technician, Operating Room Nurse. In the many interdisciplinary quality assurance committees existing in a

appearance – Erscheinung, **divisions** – Abschnitte, **to differ** – unterschiedlich sein, **ongoing** – fortlaufend, **the patient's response** – Reaktion des Patienten/das Pflegeergebnis, **to depend** – abhängig sein, **to adjust** – anpassen, **to compare** – vergleichen, **to reach** – erreichen, **bed sore prevention** – Dekubitusprophylaxe, **to indicate** – anzeigen, **to agree** – übereinstimmen, **to achieve** – erreichen, **procedures** – Methoden, **exchange** – Austausch, **takes place** – ergibt sich

hospital nursing is represented by appropriate specialty nurses who contribute from a nursing point of view to the improvement of care.

5.2.8 Patient Satisfaction and Complaints

It has been my experience that patients very often sent in »thank you notes« after their discharge stating their satisfaction with nursing care in general, or singling out a certain nurse they were particulary happy with.
However, inspite of this pleasant mail there is always room for improvement. Therefore, nurses frequently hand out questionnaires to patients and relatives in order to find out about their satisfaction with nursing. These questionnaires are very detailed as to specific aspects of nursing care. The idea behind this is to identify certain areas where nursing care can be improved and thereby contribute to the overall quality of care.

Occasionally it does happen that patients have complaints about a specific aspect of care or a situation they experience negatively. If the RN assigned to the patient is unable to solve the problem she will pass it on to the head nurse. If she is unable to take care of the situation, the nursing supervisor with her wide range of administrative possibilities usually solves the case.

Patients do not necessarily have to talk to the staff on the nursing floor when they feel the need to register a complaint. There is a telephone number given in their information booklet by which they can contact a consumer relations representative 24 hours a day (see chapter 3, Patient Information Booklet, Your Rights).
Generally, patient complaints are viewed by the persons responsible as an opportunity for the hospital to get to know about quality deficiencies and consequently to find ways to eliminate them.

to single out – hervorheben, **satisfaction** – Zufriedenheit, **it does happen** – es kommt vor, **to experience** – erleben, **to solve** – lösen, **administrative possibilities** – Managementmöglichkeiten, **to register a complaint** – eine Beschwerde vorbringen, **consumer relations representative** – Mitarbeiter der hausinternen Patientenanlaufstelle, **to view** – betrachten, **opportunity** – Gelegenheit, **deficiences** – Mängel, **to eliminate** – aufarbeiten

6 The Employment

In diesem Kapitel wird die Einführung neuer Mitarbeiter in das Krankenhaus erläutert. Es werden die vom Krankenhaus den neuen Mitarbeitern schriftlich zugesicherten Leistungen sowie die vom Krankenhaus an die neuen Mitarbeiter gestellten Anforderungen beschrieben. Bestimmte Aspekte aus den speziellen Einführungsinformationen für neue pflegerische Mitarbeiter werden aufgezeigt.

6.1 Orientation of New Employees

Hospitals have certain rules and regulations applicable to all employees. At the time of employment all new employees undergo an orientation period. This means they spend, depending on their employee category, from 1–4 weeks in the classroom before they work in their respective departements. The idea behind this is, that a proper orientation will prevent mistakes being made on the part of the new employee which may not only be costly in the monetary sense but also in creating negative publicity for the hospital.

6.1.1 The Employee Handbook

During orientation time the new employees are given general information about the work rules of the hospital and some specific instructions about their particular area of work. All receive the *Employee Handbook* which contains the rules and benefits applying to their employment.

Representative for Employment Rules and Regulations in American hospitals the Emlpoyee Handbook of St. John's Hospital in Springfield, Illinois, is introduced here. It contains six different sections. Following, these sections are listed and certain selected items in these sections are looked at:

6.1.1.1 Section 1 Purpose

This section begins with giving the history of the hospital, the mission statement and the philosophy (see chapter 3). It also states that the purpose of having and handing out the written rules and regulations in form of this handbook is to *»promote an understanding of the expectations of employment at St. John's. The hospital seeks to provide employees with fair and competitive wage and salary administration, benefit programs and a work environment con-*

applicable – betreffend, **employees** – Mitarbeiter, **employment** – Einstellung, **orientation period** – Einführungszeit, **in the monetary sense** – im geldlichen Sinn, **rules** – Regeln, **to apply** – anwenden, zutreffen, **representative** – stellvertretend, **selected** – ausgewählt, **promote** – fördern, **expectations** – Erwartungen, **to seek** – danach streben, **wage and salary administration** – Lohn und Gehaltpolitik, **ben-efit programs** – Zusatzleistungsprogramme, **work environment** – Arbeitsumfeld

ducive to quality patient care. Employees are expected to demonstrate a sincere interest in the patient's welfare, a seriousness of purpose and a friendly, cooperative spirit, in keeping with the philosophy and mission of the hospital.«

For the purpose of fostering positive employment relationsships the hospital will endeavor to:
»Respect the individual rights and dignity of employees;
Recognize the worth and importance of every job required in the operation of the hospital;
Keep the staff informed regarding policy and programs;
Provide various ways for employees to express their concerns and make suggestions;
Provide orientation and training as may be necessary for the continued competency in work performance;
Provide opportunities for employee self-development.« (page 8)

6.1.1.2 Section 2 Employment

6.1.1.2.1 Certification, Licensing, Registration

Of the several items in this section the statement about Certification, Licensing and Registration is selected and looked at since it especially affects nurses. It reads: *»Employees in certain positions are required by accrediting and licensing agencies to achieve and maintain professional certification, licensure and/registration* (see chapter 4, Licensures). *It is the responsibility of the employee to meet such standards and to notify his/her immediate manager on a continuing basis that requirements are being met and records are up-to-date, including the renewal of professional licenses«* (page 19).

6.1.1.3 Section 3 Compensation

6.1.1.3.1 Base Rate of Pay

»Base rate of pay is defined as the employee's rate of pay within the assigned pay grade for the employee's assigned job classification« (page 32). For instance: There are certain pay scale parameters in nursing depending on education, qualification and experience of registered nurses. Nurses who recently passed their state boards are beginners in nursing and are therefore paid on the lowest point of the pay scale for registered nurses. Gradually, as they increase

to expect – erwarten, **to demonstrate** – zeigen, **welfare** – Wohlergehen, **seriousness of purpose** – Ernsthaftigkeit für ihre Aufgaben, **in keeping with** – im Einklang mit, **to foster** – hegen, **employment relationships** – Anstellungsverhältnisse, **to endeavor** – sich bemühen, **worth and importance** – Wert und Bedeutung, **operation of the Hospital** – Krankenhausbetrieb, **regarding policy and programs** – bezüglich (Krankenhaus-)Zielsetzung und Programmen, **to express** – ausdrücken, **suggestions** – Vorschläge, **opportunities** – Gelegenheiten, **self-development** – Selbstentwicklung, **accrediting and licencing agencies** – Akkreditierungs- und Lizenzierungsbehörden, **to meet such standards** – diese Standards zu erfüllen, **immediate** – direkt, **records** – Unterlagen, **renewal** – Erneuerung, **compensation** – Vergütung, **base rate of pay** – Grundgehalt, **within the assigned pay grade** – innerhalb der festgelegten Gehaltsgrenzen, **pay scale parameters** – Gehaltstufen, **depending** – abhängig, **recently** – vor kurzem, **state boards** – Staatsexamen

their professional knowledge and practical experience they can advance to higher steps in the pay scale.

6.1.1.3.2 Overtime

»An employee … will be paid for overtime hours worked at least one and one-half time the base rate of pay« (page 32). This means that employees will be paid for overtime hours the amount of their base rate salary plus 50 % thereof, i.e. If a person earns $ 10.00 per hour he/she will be paid $ 15 per hour overtime (see above base rate of pay). If the overtime is worked on the afternoon or night shift, the shift differential will be added. If the person works in a charge position additional pay will be added for taking charge.

*6.1.1.3.3 **Pay Periods** and Pay Days*

»A pay period begins with the first scheduled shift on Sunday and ends with the night shift 14 consecutive days later.« Therefore, one pay period equals 2 weeks. *»Pay days are scheduled for every other Thursday«* (page 35). This means each employee's salary is deposited into his/her bank account every other Thursday. Only actual hours worked are paid. (The system of the two week pay periods is not special to hospitals but is practised in industry and other types of work in the United States.)

6.1.1.3.4 Performance Evaluation

»Each employee will be periodically evaluated to determine job proficiency. Criteria based performance evaluations are completed by the immediate manager and reviewed with the employee. The evaluation is used to discuss performance, establish objectives, clarify expectations, commend for a job well done and cite areas for improvement. It is also used when considering an employee for transfer, promotion or salary adjustment. Evaluation criteria include:

- *quality/quantitiy of work,*
- *knowledge and skills,*
- *relationships with others/communications,*
- *attendance/reliability*
- *other behavioral factors.*

New, transferred or promoted employees will receive a performance evaluation after three months of continuous employment, after 12 months of continuous employment and at least annually thereafter. Each employee may receive a percentage of his/her current base hourly rate of pay (see above base rate of pay) *upon completion of 12 months in the position. The employee will be considered*

to advance – fortschreiten, **overtime** – Überstunden, **shift differential** – Schichtzulage, **charge position** – stellvertretend für Stationsschwester, **pay periods** – Gehaltsperioden, **to schedule** – festlegen, **pay days** – Zahltage, **salary** – Gehalt, **to deposit** – einzahlen, **actual hours worked** – tatsächlich gearbeitete Stunden, **to determine** – feststellen, **job proficiency** – Arbeitskompetenz-/leistung, **performance evaluation** – Leistungsbewertung, **to review** – durchgehen/durchsprechen, **to establish objectives** – Ziele setzen, **to clarify expectations** – Erwartungen klären, **to commend** – loben, **to cite** – aufzeigen, **transfer** – Wechsel, **promotion** – Beförderung, **salary adjustment** – Gehaltserhöhung, **attendance** – Anwesenheit, **reliability** – Verlässlichkeit, **behavior** – Verhalten

for additional salary increases every 12 months until the hourly wage reaches the maximum of the salary range of his/her job.« (page 41)
Performance evaluations are done on the basis of established measurable work performance criteria and the utilization of the position descriptions available for all categories of employees.

6.1.1.3.5 Rest and Meal Periods

»St. John's provides a paid rest period of 20 minutes for each eight hour shift worked … An employee working a shift of 7 hours or more will be scheduled … for a meal period of one-half hour. … Meal time is not included in paid hours of employment« (page 30).

6.1.1.4 Section 4 Benefits

6.1.1.4.1 Employee Educational Development

»The hospital encourages employees to develop their skills and abilities to mutually benefit themselves and the hospital. St. John's offers an environment for health care education through its facilities, professionally trained staff and affiliation with Southern Illinois University School of Medicine. Educational training courses, internships and clinical training are offered in several health care fields through the hospital which also sponsors continuing education for health care professionals.
The hospital's Health Science Library provides electronic and print books and journals, reference service, interlibrary loan and scheduling of audio/visual equipment for employees, medical staff and students (see chapter 4, Inservice education).
*An employee who is required by the immediate manager to attend a short course or seminar will have resonable expenses paid by the hospital« (*page 61).

6.1.1.4.2 Tuition Reimbursement

»To be eligible for tuition reimbursement, an employee must be scheduled to work at least 32 hours per pay period (see pay period above) *and must do so for the entire academic term during which the course is scheduled. … Upon satisfactory completion of the course, a 100 % reimbursement of tuition costs will be made to the employee. … The maximum tuition reimbursement per calender year for an employee working 68–80 hours per pay period is $ 1500, for employees working 48–63 hours per pay period, the annual maximum amount is $ 1000«* (page 62).

maximum of the salary range – höchste Gehaltsstufe in einer bestimmten Gehaltskategorie, **utilization** – Einsatz, **position descriptions** – Tätigkeitsbeschreibungen, **to schedule** – einteilen, **to include** – einschließen, **paid hours** – bezahlte Stunden, **to encourage** – ermuntern, **mutual benefit** – wechselseitiger Nutzen, **to offer** – anbieten, **health care education** – Gesundheitserziehung, **affiliation** – Anschluss, **continuing education** – Fortbildung, **library** – Bibliothek, **reference service** – Nachschlagdienste, **to require** – auffordern, **to attend** – teilnehmen, **reasonable expenses** – angemessene Kosten, **eligible** – berechtigt, **tuition reimbursement** – Studiengebührenerstattung, **entire** – gesamt, **satisfactory completion** – erfolgreicher Abschluss

6.1.1.4.3 Employee of the Month, of the Year Award

»*The employee of the Month/Year Award identifies and gives proper recognition to employees who consistently exemplify the philosophy and mission of the hospital* (see chapter 3, Mission statement, Philosophy) *through caring behavior which fosters better relations among patients, visitors, medical staff, samaritans and employees. These employees are role models for other employees.*

The Employee of the Month Selection Committee … will make the selection based upon the relative merit of the actions or particular event for which the employee was nominated. … The selected employee will receive a written recommendation from the Executive Vice President, with copies filed in the employees's personal file and the supervisor's file. A plaque bearing the photograph of the Employee of the Month will be appropriately displayed in the hospital cafeteria and an individual plaque will be provided to the employee and the department head for posting it in the employee's department. In addition, the selected employee will receive free reserved parking for one month and a monetary reward.

An employee of the Year will be chosen from among 12 Employees of the Month at the end of each year. The nominee whose performance and positive attitude are considered to most highly examplify the hospital's standards and core values and who would best be identified as a role model for all employees will be selected by vote of the committee.
The Employee of the Year will receive a commendation from the Executive Vice President, will be featured in the cafeteria and the department plaques and receive an individual plaque. In addition, the Employee of the Year will receive: One year free reserved parking; a wristwatch bearing the hospital's logo with an inscription designating – Employee of the Year – and a monetary reward. All Employees of the Month and their spouses or a guest will be invited to a dinner with the Administration Team and Personnel Director« (page 63).

6.1.1.4.4 Holidays

The following are recognized paid holidays of the hospital:

New Year's Day	January 1
Memorial Day	the last Monday in May
Independence Day	July 4
Labor Day	the first Monday in September
Thanksgiving Day	the last Thursday in November
Christmas Day	December 25 (page 48)

employee of the month, the year – Mitarbeiter des Monats/des Jahres, **award** – Auszeichnung, **recognition** – Anerkennung, **to consistently exemplify** – beständig verkörpern, **caring behavior** – fürsorgliches Verhalten, **relations** – Verhältnis, **samaritans** – ehrenamtliche Helfer, **role models** – Rollenvorbilder, **selection** – Auswahl, **merit** – Verdienst, **particular event** – spezieller Anlass, **executive vice president** – stellvertretender Betriebsleiter, **personal file** – Personalakte, **supervisor** – Abteilungsleitung, **plaque** – Plakette, **to display** – ausstellen, **department head** – Abteilungsleitung, **monetary reward** – monetäre Anerkennung, **nominee** – der Genannte/Ausgewählte, **most highly examplify** – am höchsten verkörpern, **core values** – zentrale Werte, **commendation** – Belobigung, **inscription** – Inschrift, **spouses** – Ehegatten, **paid holidays** – bezahlte Feiertage

6.1.1.4.5 Paid Time Off/Vacation

»The Paid Time Off = PTO-Programm combines time off with pay into one category, which is the PTO balance. Time off may include vacation, personal time, recognized holidays and sick time …(see Earned Illness Benefit below). It recognizes and meets the needs of employees for greater flexibility in taking time off. It also empowers employees to assume responsibility for managing their own time off from work …

Accrual of PTO is based upon length of continuous service and actual hours paid, up to 2080 hours per calender year.

Table of Accrual

Length of Service	Maximum Annual Accrual
0– 4 years	25 days = 200 hours
5–10 years	30 days = 240 hours
11 years	31 days = 248 hours
12 years	32 days = 256 hours
13 years	33 days = 264 hours
14 years	34 days = 272 hours
15 years	35 days = 280 hours

Part time employees accrue PTO on a pro-rated basis, based on hours paid per year« (page 46).
This schedule of PTO accrual is increased in hours as employees attain certain management positions.

6.1.1.4.6 Earned Illness Benefit/Sick Time

»An employee accrues eight hours (one day) of Earned Illness Benefits (EIB) time for every 260 hours of paid employment (excluding overtime and on-call time) to a maximum of 64 hours (eight days) annually …
Employees may use EIB after 90 calender days of employment.
During the first three scheduled days or 24 hours … that an employee is ill, PTO time must be used. Beginning with the 3rd day or the 25th hour of absence due to illness or injury, an employee may use accrued EIB time. If the employee is hospitalized or undergoes outpatient surgery which causes absence from work for more than three scheduled days or 24 hours, EIB time may be used from the first day. A physician's statement will be required to document the reason for the extended absence« (page 49).

paid time off – bezahlte Freizeit, **vacation** – Urlaub, **sick time** – Krankheitstage, **to empower** – befähigen, **to assume responsibility** – Verantwortung übernehmen, **accrual** – Ansammlung, **actual** – tatsächlich, **to attain** – erreichen, **to earn** – erwerben, **paid employment** – bezahlte Arbeitszeit, **on-call time** – Bereitschaftsdienst, **illness** – Krankheit, **injury** – Verletzung, **physician statement** – ärztliches Attest

6.1.1.4.7 Health Insurance

»Core benefits are considered essential to employee welfare and provided automatically to all employees ... These core benefits include: the basic level of medical, life and disability insurance. Each eligible employee receives the core benefits and has the option of adding to those benefits ...« with his own funds (page 44).

6.1.1.4.8 **Pension Plan**

»The Hospital Sisters Health System provides an Employee Pension Plan ... Employee coverage in the pension plan is fully paid for by the hospital.
Participation in the pension plan beginns on the January 1 or July 1 following completion of 12 consecutive months of employment in which 1000 hours or more are worked. To be vested in the pension plan (eligible to receive pension payments), an employee must work 1000 hours or more per year for five years. The number of years of service at a 1000 hours or more per year and the amount of earnings determine the amount of the pension benefit.« (page 60)
This hospital based pension plan is in addition to employees paying into the Social Security Service and receiving a pension from this nationwide federal agency.

6.1.1.5 Section 5 Customer Service/Employment Expectations

6.1.1.5.1 Customer Service

»St. John's Hospital has established a tradition of high ethical and professional standards to which employees must actively subscribe in the performance of their job duties. These standards include appropriate conduct, cooperation, efficiency and effectiveness. Managers will direct activities and staff in a manner which meets these standards and are responsible for taking corrective action if an employee's work habits, attendance/punctuality, attitude, productivity or personal conduct fall below acceptable standards ...« (page 72).
A list of examples of courteous activities with which to create »great first impressions« is given in order to help the employee to fulfill these requirements.

6.1.1.5.2 Dress Code

»St. John's is committed to professionalism, customer service and continuous improvement. In keeping with this commitment, the physical appearance/dress of employees as viewed by our customers is of primary importance. The impression made through appearance and dress will be consistent with our core values of respect, care and hospitality and will support a business-like environment.

core benefits – Kernzusatzleistungen, **disability** – Behinderung, **option** – Möglichkeit, **adding** – Dazuzahlen, **own funds** – Eigenbeteiligung, **pension plan** – Pensionsplan, **pension payments** – Pensionsauszahlungen, **years of service** – Arbeitsjahre, **amount of earnings** – Summe des Verdienstes, **Social Security Service** – staatliche Rentenversicherung, **customer** – Kunde, **to actively subscribe** – aktive mittragen, **appropriate conduct** – entsprechendes Verhalten, **in a manner** – in einer Art und Weise, **corrective Aktion** – korrektives Eingreifen, **work habits** – Arbeitsgewohnheiten, **personal conduct** – persönliches Verhalten, **courteous** – höflich, **great first impressions** – große erste Eindrücke, **to fulfill** – erfüllen, **to be committed** – verpflichtet sein, **customers** – Kunden, **impression** – Eindruck, **dress** – Kleidung, **core values** – zentrale Werte

Deparments have established policies regarding appearance and attire. Employees will be advised of the department dress code at the time of employment. The hospital reserves the right to require employees to wear uniforms while on duty (see chapter 5, Work Uniforms).
Employees who are not required to wear uniforms must present a business-like appearance by wearing clothing appropriate to their work area …« (page 85).

6.6.1.5.3 Identification Badges

Employees and others associated with the hospital must wear authorized hospital identification badges while on duty. Badges must be kept in good condition and worn at eye level so that the employee's photograph is easily visible and the name easily read (see Chapter 4, Name Tag).
Employees may wear pins or insignia directly related to the employee's vocation or profession. These may be equipped with safety clasps, guard chains or other devices to prevent loss which might result in food or drug contamination, personal injury, equipment interference, or which may disrupt patient care« (page 86).

6.6.1.5.4 Grievance Procedure

»St. Johns makes every effort to prevent conditions which may result in a grievance, and to deal promptly, properly, fairly, objectively and in good faith with the grievances which occur.
Eligible employees have the right to utilize the grievance procedure without being subjected to restraint, interference, discrimination, retaliation or harrassment of any form provided the procedure is also followed in good faith by the employee.
Definition: A grievance shall be considered to be any complaint or dissatisfaction arising from an application or claimed violation of the hospital policies, rules or regulations which may or will result in disziplinary action being taken by the hospital which the employee feels is unjust« … (page 93).
To file a grievance an employee should follow the proper steps laid down in the grievance procedure.

to reserve the right – sich vorbehalten, **duty** – Dienst, **identification badges** – Namenskarten, **insignia** – Abzeichen, **directly related** – in direktem Zusammenhang, **vocation** – Beruf, **equipped** – ausgestattet, **safety clasps** – Sicherheitsverschluss, **guard chains** – Sicherheitsketten, **contamination** – Verunreinigung, **equipment interference** – Funktionsstörung von Geräten, **to disrupt** – unterbrechen, **grievance** – Beschwerde, **in good faith** – vertrauensvoll, **to be subjected to** – ausgesetzt sein, **restraint** – Zurückhaltung, **retaliation** – Racheakt, **harrassment** – Quälereien, **provided** – vorausgesetzt, **dissatisfaction** – Unzufriedenheit, **application** – Anwendung, **claimed violation** – angebliche Nichtbeachtung, **disziplinary action** – Disziplinarmaßnahme, **unjust** – ungerecht, **to file a grievance** – eine Beschwerde einreichen

6.1.1.6 Section 6 General Information

6.1.1.6.1 **Security Services**

»The Security Deparment is available to assist employees and the public by providing escorts to automobiles, providing information and assisting in maintaining the overall security of hospital premises.
The cooperation of every employee is necessary if the hospital is to remain safe and secure. Any breach of security, presence of suspicious individuals in the hospital or any incident of theft must be reported to a security officer on duty« (page 104).

6.1.1.6.2 **Rumor Line**

»To improve communication throughout the hospital, a Rumor Line is available to address issues that are of common concern to employees and to dispel erroneous information. Any employee who has received information that is of questionable validity or of concern may telephone the Rumor Line (the number is given). This telephone line is operational 24 hours a day, seven days a week« (page 104).

The Employee Handbook with working rules and regulations, out of which selected items were presented above, is given to all employees during their orientation. In addition to this basic work information, specific information is given to persons working in specialized areas pertinent to their particular duties. One such group of persons working in different specialized areas are nurses. Following, an overview of their work specific orientation is given.

6.2 Nursing Orientation

Most hospitals have a nurse recruiter. This is an RN = Registered Nurse working in the personnel department. She conducts the first employment interviews with potentially new nurses. If she deems an applicant employable she will take the nurse to the appropriate head nurse who in turn interviews her and decides on whether or not this person should be hired for her team.
Upon employment the person begins with orientation (see chapter 4, Inservice Education).

The nursing orientation programm in the class room lasts one week, and thereafter is tailored to the individual's needs. The new nurses are given the Nursing Orientation Manual which describes the topics taught and skills trained during orientation. Although nursing in the different hospitals is practised on a similar professional standard the steps for certain pro-

security services – Sicherheitsdienste, **to assist** – unterstützen, **escort** – Begleitung, **hospital premises** – Krankenhausgelände, **breach of security** – Verletzung der Sicherheit, **suspicious** – verdächtig, **theft** – Diebstahl, **security officer** – Wachmann, **rumor line** – Gerüchteküche, **common concern** – allgemeines Interesse, **to dispel** – zerstreuen, **erroneous** – falsch, **questionable validity** – fragwürdige Richtigkeit, **overview** – Überblick, **to deem** – erachten, **applicant** – Bewerber, **employable** – einstellungsfähig, **to tailor to** – zuschneiden, **topics** – Themen, **similar** – ähnlich

cedures and the forms to document services may differ. For this reason it is necessary that new nurses are familiarized with the way things are done in their new place of employment.

6.2.1 The Nursing Orientation Manual

Representative for the Nursing Orientation Manuals used in American hospitals the Nursing Orientation Manual of Cedars Medical Center, in Maimi, Florida, is introduced. Following, the topics of this manual are listed and discussed, where necessary.

6.2.1.1 Clinical Aspects

The manual beginns with the *mission statement* and the *philosophy of nursing* (see Chapter 4, The Nursing Department).
The next topic deals with specific aspects of the *nursing process* and *nursing documentation.* Instructions for documenting the nursing process and the administration of medications are given in two ways; one way is using the paper forms, the other is using the computer.

There are several sample forms used for *physician's orders* (see chapter 5, Physician's Orders), *patient admission*, *safety*, *comfort*, *discharge* and *consent* of patients.

There are special forms based on the appropriate procedure for documenting the *safe keeping of valuables* and *dentures* of patients.

On the basis of the forms for the utilization of *side rails* and *restraints* the policy and procedure for these nursing actions are discussed (see chapter 4, Policy and Procedure).

A special form is used to document *non-compliance* of the patient.

The *discharge instruction* form reminds the nurse about the kind of information/instruction she is to give the patient prior to his discharge from the hospital and how to document this nursing task.

The legal background for *advanced directives or living wills* is given and a sample form to be used by the patient and witnesses is included.

Samples of frequently used nursing forms such as *intake and output, diabetic flow sheets, neurological check lists, heparin administration* and *pre-operative check lists* are given.

to differ – unterschiedlich sein, **to familiarize** – bekannt machen, **instructions** – Anweisungen, **administration** – Vergabe, **forms** – Formulare, **sample** – Muster, **physician's order** – ärztliche Verordnungen, **patient admission** – Patientenaufnahme, **comfort** – Wohlergehen, **discharge** – Entlassung, **safe keeping of valuables** – Verwahrung von Wertsachen, **dentures** – Zahnprotesen, **side rails** – Bettgitter, **restraints** – Sicherungsgurte, **non-compliance** – Mitarbeitsverweigerung, **task** – Aufgabe, **legal background** – rechtlicher Hintergrund, **advanced directives or living will** – Patientenverfügung, **witness** – Zeuge

In addition to standard nursing forms certain interdisciplinary procedures are discussed with the newly employed nurses and the appropriate forms shown, i.e. procedure for *blood transfusion, infection control, AIDS testing* and *medication administration*.

6.2.1.2 Emergencies

In case of emergencies certain code words are used to alert the designated emergency teams. These code words and appropriate nursing action in case of emergencies are discussed:
CODE RED is the code word for emergencies like fire, bomb threat or an unusual influx of emergency patients (see chapter 4, Inservice, Required Education). The necessity for the periodically held emergency exercises are explained.
CODE BLUE is the code word for an emergency in which there is a life threatening situation for a particular patient. In case of a Code Blue the nurse responsible for the patient will initiate resuscitation until the arrival of a physician and the cardio-pulmonary team.
On this topic the manual contains the form for documentation of the cardio-pulmonary resuscitation process. In addition, there is a graphic lay out of the crash cart, showing the standard content of each drawer of the cart which is identical on all nursing floors.
Depending on the patient's diagnosis and condition the physician may write the order: Do Not Resuscitate = DNR. This means for the nurse(s) that no resuscitation is to be carried out. The patient is nursed palliatively until his death.
A DNR order will also be written by the physician in cases where the patient has given written advanced directives = a living will. Nursing care is the same as above.

These code words are used in all hospitals. Both emergencies are announced via the hospital intercom system. In both emergencies standard procedures are carried out by the designated emergency teams.

6.2.1.3 Getting help

There are certain complex situations in nursing in which nurses need clinical help and advice. Therefore, nurses are given information in which work situations they can and should ask for help from the Clinical Nurse Specialist (see Chapter 4, Nursing personnel). For instance:
»When confronted with a crisis,
when assistance is needed to fine-tune the assessment, nursing diagnoses, planning and evaluation of patient care,
when dealing with a new disease process or unfamiliar aspect of patient care,
when developing unit specific or patient population-specific nursing standards,
when evaluating new products or equipment,
when planning new services« (page 54).

medication administration – Arzneimittelvergabe, **designated** – beauftragen, **bomb threat** – Bombendrohung, **influx** – Zustrom, **exercise** – Übung, **life threatening** – lebensbedrohlich, **resuscitation** – reanimieren, **crash cart** – Notfallwagen, **drawer** – Schublade, **living will** – Patientenverfügung, **to announce** – ausrufen, **advice** – Rat, **assistance** – Unterstützung, **to fine tune** – differenzieren, **disease** – Krankheit, **unfamiliar** – unbekannt, **unit** – Station, **patient-population** – Patientengruppe

6.2.1.4 Professional opportunity

In this section the Clinical Ladder **System** is explained. A clinical ladder is an advancement system for RNs = Registered Nurses working at the bedside. Based on the acquisition of specific educational knowledge and work skills over a two year period RNs can apply for promotion to the next higher level in the ladder. The clinical ladder committee, consisting of nurses and nurse educators (all RNs) will evaluate the application on the basis of established criteria and approve or disapprove the advancment. An approved advancement means added status and a monetary increase for the nurse.

clinical ladder – klinische Leiter, **advancement** – Aufstieg, **acquisition** – Erwerb, **knowledge** – Wissen, **to consist of** – bestehend aus, **monetary increase** – Gehaltserhöhung

7 The Nursing Education

In diesem Kapitel werden die unterschiedlichen Möglichkeiten einer pflegerischen Bildung von der untersten bis zur höchsten Stufe gezeigt. Es werden verschiedene Bildungsstätten aufgelistet. Die hauptsächlich an der Sicherstellung der Bildungsqualität involvierten beruflichen Selbstverwaltungsorgane werden skizziert. Ein typisches Studienprogramm für den Erwerb eines Bachelor Grades in der Pflege wird vorgestellt.

7.1 Ways of Nursing Education

Over the past decades nursing education has been expanded and diversified and several different educational structures have evolved. Currently there are many different ways for nursing education. Of the different ways in which nursing education takes place two main tracks can be identified. One is the usual **way**, the others are **unusual ways.**

7.1.1 The Usual Way

Starting on the lowest level of the educational scale is the *Practical* or *Vocational Nurse*. This type of nursing education takes place at vocational or trade schools, or at hospital affiliated schools for the duration of 12 months. It is comparable to the German Schwesternhelferin-Ausbildung (see Fig. 12).

The next step up is the nurse educated in a 3 year program at a hospital affiliated Diploma School. This is the traditional way of educating a *Registered Nurse.* This type of nursing education is similar to the German Krankenschwester/Krankenpfleger.

On the same formal level is the *Associate Degree Nurse.* This type of nursing education takes place at colleges for the duration of 2 years. Its purpose is to educate technically oriented nurses who can assist the Registered Nurses.

Both these kinds of education lead to the national examination for becoming a professional nurse. By passing the examination the title of *Registered Nurse* = RN is obtained. Registered Nurse signifies that the person has been admitted to the register of qualified professional nurses maintained by the State Board of Nursing in each State of the United States. Persons thus educated and examined can work as RNs.

education – Bildung, **to expand** – erweitern, **to diversify** – differenzieren, **to evolve** – herausbilden, **tracks** – Richtungen, **usual** – üblich, **vocational or trade schools** – Berufsfachschulen, **hospital affiliated** - mit einem Krankenhaus verbunden, **to signify** – zeigen, **State Board of Nursing** – Pflegekammer, **thus** – auf diese Weise

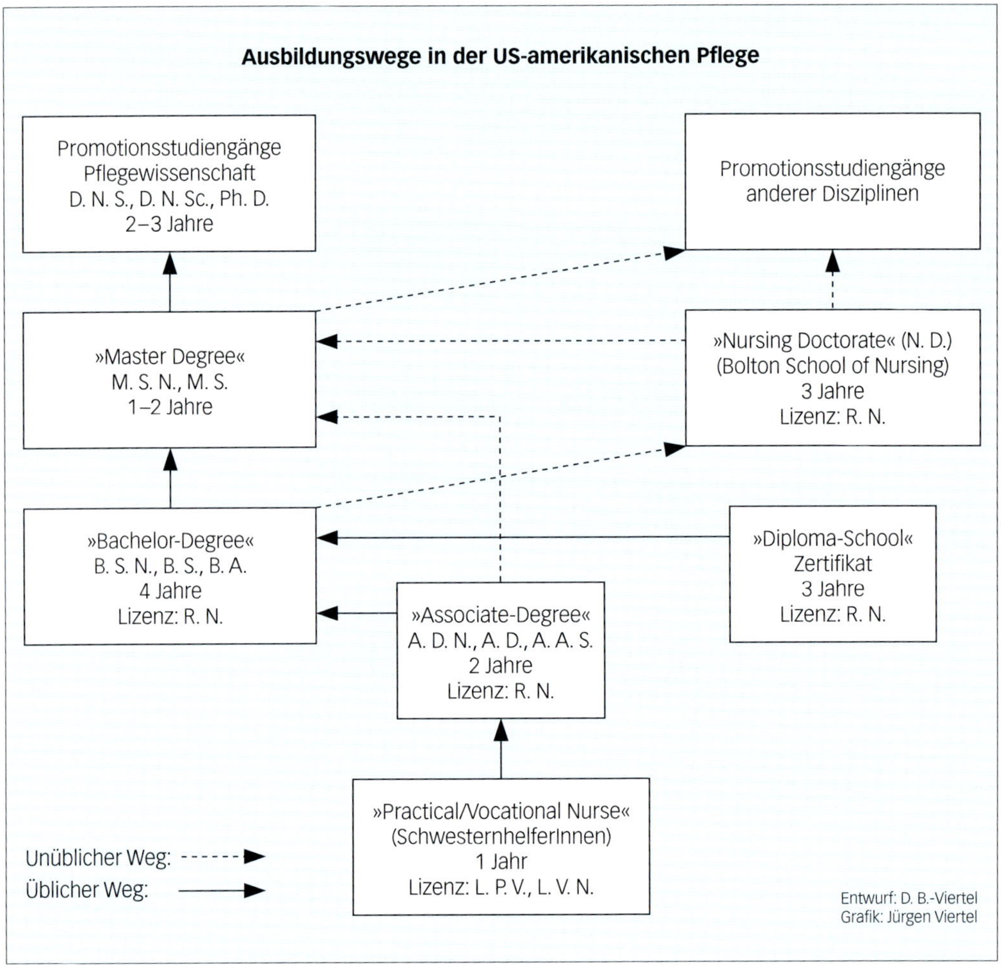

Fig. 12: Ausbildungswege in den USA. Mit freundlicher Genehmigung D. Buckley-Viertel, 2001.

If these persons wish to expand their professional knowledge they can enter a *Bachelor Degree* Program. As a rule, credit is given for previous nursing studies and practical experience. Of course, there is also the possibility to enter a Bachelor Degree Programm directly without going through the so far described channels.

The Bachelor Degree Program is a 4-year educational process at a university. During the first two years teaching is oriented on the liberal arts, natural science and socio-cultural aspects. The second two years deal with nursing science. Students in this program have to pass their academic exams **and** the national examination for becoming a professional nurse.

Bachelor Degree – 1. Universitätsgrad, **as a rule** – gewöhnlich, **credit** – Anerkennung, **previous nursing studies** – vorhergegangene Pflegestudien, **channels** – Känale/Wege, **liberal arts** – Geisteswissenschaften, **natural science** – Naturwissenschaften, **nursing science** – Pflegewissenschaft

The product of this kind of education is the *Registered Nurse with a Bachelor Degree in Nursing = RN, BSN.*

The next step up is the *Master Degree in Nursing.* Studying for a Master Degree in Nursing means specialization in a certain field of nursing in preparation for becoming a Clinical Nurse Specialist. For instance, there are Clinical Nurse Specialists in Oncology, Medical-Surgical Nursing, Orthopedics, Child Care, Public Health and many others. The study time required to obtain a Master degree in Nursing = MSN is 1–2 years (see chapter 4, Nursing Personnel).
After the completion of the bachelor and master degree in nursing the nurse has the titles RN, BSN, MSN.

The next step is the *Doctoral Degree in Nursing.* These studies based on a the Master Degree place emphasis on statistics, research and theory development. Study time required is 4–6 semesters.

The steps described so far show the usual way of nursing education.

7.1.2 The Unusual Ways

Unusual ways for education in nursing are to go from a Bachelor Degree to a Nursing Doctorate, or from an Associate Degree to a Master Degree. It is also possible to go from a Nursing Doctorate to a Master Degree. There is also the possibility to go from a Master Degree in Nursing or a Nursing Doctorate to a Doctorate in other disciplines. (For a detailed description of the different ways of nursing education see Buckley-Viertel, 2001.)

7.1.3 Institutions for Nursing Education

There are 4 different institutions for nursing education:

1. The Trade School, the Vocational School and the hospital affiliated Hospital School for Practical or Vocational Nurses.
2. The hospital affiliated Nursing School for Registered Nurses.
3. The College, issuing an Associate Degree in Nursing.
4. The University, issuing a Bachelor, a Master and a Doctoral Degree in Nursing.

Based on the demand for academic education in nursing many US universities have implemented nursing education programs. Whether or nor a university does have a nursing education program can be found out by checking the lecture catalog.

In this context it is noteworthy that the departments of a university are called School of … For instance, University of Colorado, School of Architecture; or University of Colorado, School of Education; or University of Colorado, School of Nursing. The term *School of Nurs-*

Master Degree – 2. Universitätsgrad, **preparation** – Vorbereitung, **to obtain** – erwerben, **based on** – aufbauend, **unusual** – ungewöhnlich, **to issue** – herausgeben/verleihen, **demand** – Nachfrage, **lecture catalog** – Vorlesungsverzeichnis, **noteworthy** – erwähnenswert

ing has nothing to do with our idea of school of nursing in the sense of a hospital affiliated diploma school. The term *school* is generally used to name the different sections within a university.

7.1.4 Quality of Nursing Education

The National League for Nursing = NLN is the official professional accrediting organization for master, baccalaureate (Bachelor), associate degree, diploma and practical nurse programs in the United States (see Fig. 12 Ausbildungswege). The accrediting process is carried out by four NLN councils: The Council of Baccalaureate and Higher Degree Programs, the Council of Associate Degree Programs, the Council of Diploma Programs, the Council of Practical Nurse Programs. These accrediting programs with their specific criteria are developed by each council and periodically revised. The established criteria for each accrediting program are outcome criteria (see Kittrell Chitty, 1997).

All nursing education programs must also be accredited by the State Board of Nursing in their respective States. »*Accreditation refers to a voluntary review process of educational programs by a professional organization. The organization, called an accrediting agency, compares the educational quality of the program with established standards and criteria. Accrediting agencies derive their authority from the US Department of Education*« (Kittrell Chitty, 1997: 46).

The purpose of accrediting nursing education programs is to maintain a certain standard of quality in nursing education. It is further to insure quality nursing care for the public and safety in professional work. And lastly, it assures nursing students that their educational program offers quality education.
Review of a once accredited nursing program takes place every 8 years. In case of deficiencies in the program the educational instituion receives a warning and a time period in which correction has to take place. Accreditation can be withdrawn if deficiencies are not corrected within the given time.

Contributing to the quality of a nursing education programm is the educational qualification of the lecturers and professors teaching in the nursing department. In order to show the educational qualification of the teaching personnel the lecture catalog lists in alphabetical order all names of lecturers and professors, their academic qualifications and the names of Universities at which these qualifications were obtained. For instance, Charron, Sue Ann, Associate Professor of Nursing, BSN, Wayne State University; MSN, Emory University; PhD, University of Michigan (see Barry University, Undergraduate Catalog 2000/2001).

hospital affiliated – dem Krankenhaus angeschlossen, **accrediting organization** – anerkennende Behörde, **to revise** – überarbeiten, **outcome criteria** – Ergebniskriterien, **State Board of Nursing** – Pflegekammer, **voluntary review** – freiwillige Überprüfung, **to compare** – vergleichen, **to derive** – ableiten, **purpose** – Zweck, **to insure** – sicherstellen, **once accredited** – einmal anerkannt, **deficiency** – Unzulänglichkeit, **to withdraw** – entziehen, **to contribute** – beitragen, **to obtain** – erwerben

7.1.5 An Academic Study Program

Since academically educated nurses are in the majority and their number continuously increasing (see G. Taylor in: Buckley-Viertel, 2001) a typical study program for obtaining a bachelor of nursing degree is shown below using the lecture catalog of Barry University in Miami, Florida, 2000/2001.

7.1.5.1 Mission Statement

Corresponding with the overall Mission Statement of Barry University the Mission Statement of the School of Nursing reads: »*The purpose of the undergraduate nursing program is to offer students a baccalaureate education which will prepare them, in the milieu of a caring environment, for professional nursing practice. The program, within a basic Judeo-Christian humanistic framework, aims to lay a foundation for safe nursing practice, the progression to positions that require administrative skills without additional education, beginning skills in research, continued personal and professional growth, and graduate studies in nursing.*«

7.1.5.2 Philosophy

In accordance with the overall Philosophy of Barry University the Philosophy of the School of Nursing reads: »*This philosophy describes the beliefs of the faculty of the Barry University School of Nursing about persons, environment, health, illness, professional nursing, and professional nursing education.*
The faculty believes that humans are unique beings who have intrinsic value endowed in them by the Creator. Humans manifest a mind-body-spirit unity. This unity is expressed in multidimensional unfoldings which encourage creativity, harmony, and health. The essence of this human unity is dynamically situated in the individual's context, culture, environment and changing contingencies. We respect the diversity, multiple realities, and individual choices of all persons. Within the context of caring we place value on the quality of life for human beings.«

7.1.5.3 Objectives

The objectives of the baccalaureate program in nursing are to enable students to:

»• *utilize the health process to improve health care,*
- *utilize the communication process with clients, families, and members of the health team in providing nursing care,*
- *utilize critical thinking in planning and delivering health care,*
- *utilze leadership/management processes in health care delivery,*
- *utilize the nursing process with clients, including individuals, families, groups and communities,*
- *demonstrate professional behavior in the performance of nursing practice,*

corresponding – einhergehend, **caring environment** – fürsorgliches Umfeld, **framework** – Rahmenkonzept, **to aim** – abzielen, **progression** – Hinführung, to require – erfordern, **beginning skills** – Anfangskenntnisse, **graduate studies** – Studien nach Erwerb des Bachelorgrades, **belief** – Annahme, **illness** – Erkrankung, **unique** – einmalig, **to endow** – verleihen, **unfoldings** – Entfaltungen, **situated** – eingebettet, **changing contingencies** – wechselnde Möglichkeiten, **diversity** – Vielfalt, **choice** – Auswahlmöglichkeit, **objectives** – Ziele, **to utilize** – einsetzen/nutzen, **behavior** – Verhalten

- *utilize the research process to improve nursing practice, and*
- *utilize the teaching/learning process in providing nursing care and promoting health.«*

7.1.5.4 Content

The lecture catalog describes the different ways and corresponding study requirements for the obtainment of a bachelor degree in nursing. Students can chose to go from an LPN education or an RN education to a bachelor of nursing, or they can take accelerated programs which require previous studies and/or degrees. Following, a classical four year study course to obtain a bachelor of nursing degree is introduced.

The four year study course consists of a
Lower Division – during which *Pre-Nursing Requirements* must be fulfilled, and an
Upper Division – during which *Specific Nursing Requirements* must be fulfilled.

In order for the student to progress from the Lower Division to the Upper Division the following study courses have to be successfully completed.

Lower Division – Pre-Nursing Requirements:
- English Composition and Research,
- Fundamentals of Speech,
- Introductory Human Anatomy- with lab*,
- Introductory Human Physiology- with lab,
- Introductory Microbiology- with lab,
- Introductory Organic and Biological Chemestry- with lab
- Elementary Probability and Statistics
- Introduction to Psychology,
- Any History, Economics, Geography, Political Science-selectable,
- Any Anthropology or Sociology- selectable,
- Philosophy Distribution,
- Biomedical Ethics,
- Theology Distribution,
- Any Social Science Distribution- selectable,
- Any Humanities and Arts Distribution- selectable,
- Nutrition in Clinical Care,
- Introduction to Computers,
- Open Elective.

Having completed these pre-nursing courses the student transfers to the Upper Division to begin fulfilling the Specific Nursing Requirements.

* lab = Übungsraum

to promote – fördern, **corresponding** – entsprechend, **requirements** – Anforderungen, **obtainment** – Erwerb, **to accelerate** – beschleunigen, **to successfully complete** – erfolgreich abschließen, **composition** – Aufsatz, **to introduce** – einführen, **selectable** – wahlweise, **nutrition** – Ernährung, **open elective** – Wahlfächer

Upper Division – Specific Nursing Requirements:
- Introduction to Professional Nursing,
- Pharmacology,
- Foundational Concepts of Health and Health Assessment,
- Adult Health Nursing,
- Research in Nursing,
- Parent/Newborn Nursing,
- Child/Adolescent Nursing,
- Adult/Elderly Nursing:Biophysical Concepts,
- Adult/Elderly Nursing:Mental Health Nursing,
- Community Health Nursing,
- Nursing Management.

To orient students to the content of these courses an abstract is given for each. The credit points applied to theory and clinical practice for each course are shown. Following are two samples of abstracts of two different courses. The credit point system is explained below.

Adult Health Nursing – Theory 3, Clinical 4;
Focuses on nursing care of the adult health client with psychosocial and patho-physiological alternations in the major body systems. Health assessment skills are further developed to recognize abnormal findings and correlate these data to disease process to develop a plan of care. Clinical and laboratory experience is included (prerequisite courses).

Community Health Nursing – Theory 3, Clinical 3;
Focuses on health promotion and illness prevention, synthesis and application of nursing skills and theory while caring for individuals, families and aggregates as an integral part of the community. Students study public health principles, and experience an in-depth relationship with client(s) over an extended period of time in a variety of community settings to become familiar with the many roles of the community health nurse (prerequisite courses).

At the end of each abstract prerequisite courses are listed. This is to let the student know which courses must be taken prior to taking this course. The total study program is modularized.

7.1.5.5 Credit Points

As seen above, credit points are shown for each study course. These can differ from 1–5 and more credit points. If a course requires, as shown in the above examples, *3 credit points Theory*, this means: the student is in class *3 hours per week* during each semester week.
The *4 or 3 credit points Clinical* means, the student is in the clinical field, in the above examples in the hospital or in the community, *4 or 3 hours per week* during each semester week.

foundational concepts – grundlegende Konzepte, **adult** – Erwachsene, **adolescent** – Jugendliche, **credit points applied** – gegebene Punktwerte, **samples** – Muster/Beispiele, **alternations** – Veränderungen, **to correlate** – verbinden, **prerequisite courses** – vorab erforderliche Kurse, **aggregates** – Gruppen/Gemeinden, **in-depth relationship** – vertieftes Verhältnis, **to extend** – verlängern, **prior** – vor

The study program described here calls for fulfillment of the following total amount of credits:
Total credits for The Lower Division are 71 credits.
Total credits for the Upper Division are 56–58 credits.

On the basis of *course content* and *course credits* the student can change from one academic institution to another and have her/his academic work accepted by the institution she/he is transferring to.

Credit points assigned to each study course enable the student to arrange and organize a study program compatible with her/his prevailing life circumstances. This is especially important for students who study part time while holding a full time job, caring for family and having a multitude of responsibilities. Based on the total credits required the time necessary for obtaining the desired degree can be calculated. Generally, there are three semesters in one academic year.

7.1.5.6 Grading System

At the end of each course, which is the end of the semester, the student has to pass an examination which can take different forms: Oral or written tests, homework, presentations, others. A grade is given for individual performance. The scale of the grading system is the exact opposite to the one used in Germany, as can be seen in the following example:

Grade A = 4 = excellent
Grade B = 3 = good
Grade C = 2 = average
Grade D = 1 = poor
Grade F = 0 = failure

7.1.5.7 Finances

Usually, institutions of higher learning require tuition payments from students. The amount to be paid at state subsidized universities is considerably less than at private universities. It differs from one university to another. Nurses working at health care institutions and studying part time can expect a certain amount of tuition reimbursement from their place of employment (see chapter 6, Benefits).

to transfer – wechseln, **prevailing** – vorherrschend, **circumstances** – Umstände, **responsibility** – Verantwortung, **to obtain** – erwerben, **grade** – Note, **performance** – Leistung, **scale** – Stufen, **exact opposite** – genaue Gegenteil, **tuition payments** – Studiengebühren, **state subsidized** – staatlich subventioniert, **considerable** – beachtlich, **tuition reimbursement** – Vergütung der Studiengebühren

Appendix

Professional Nursing Organizations in the United States

American Nurses Organizations/Associations declare the purpose of their work as serving the public, the profession of nursing, and the individual nurse. »*They serve the public by establishing codes of ethics and standards of practice, socializing new members to these codes and standards, and enforcing codes and standards in practice. These measures, when combined with state licensure laws, assure the public that nurses are competent professionals with safe standards of practice and appropriate ethical beliefs*« (*Kittrell Chitty* 1997: 89).

There are numerous nursing organizations/associations in the United States. Generally, they can be divided into three categories:

1. Broad purpose professional associations.
2. Specialty practice associations.
3. Special interest associations.

The American Nurses Association

The ANA is a **broad purpose association** in nursing. The ANA is a federation consisting of 53 state associations. The goal of the ANA is to:

- »work for the improvement of health standards and the availability of health care services for all people (see chapter 4, Quality patient care),
- foster high standards for nursing,
- stimulate and promote the professional development of nurses and advance their economic and general welfare.« (Kittrell Chitty, 1997: 94)

Of the numerous activities carried out by the ANA to support nurses in the practice field is professional guidance in situations for which no adequate legal decision making mechanisms are available. For these situations the organization has developed and issued an Ethical Code for Nurses (see chapter 4, Nursing Ethics). The idea is to give nurses ethical orientation in difficult professional situations. In addition to the broad statements of the code specific directions for the handling of particular ethical issues are published.

code – Codex, **state licensure laws** – staatliche Lizenzierungsgesetze, **safe standards** – sicheren Standards, **ethical beliefs** – ethischen Einstellungen, **numerous** – zahlreich, **broad purpose** – breit angelegt, **federation** – Zusammenschluss, **availability** – Verfügbarkeit, **foster** – fördern, **to advance** – vorwärtsbringen, **to carry out** – durchführen, **guidance** – Führung, **adequate legal decision making mechanisms** – ausreichende rechtliche Entscheidungsmechanismen, **difficult** – schwierig, **directions** – Hinweise

Specialty practice **associations** recruit their members from particular nursing specialties, such as cardiology, critcal care, oncology, community nursing and many others. These organizations are concerned with standards of practice in that specialty only and with the particular needs of that group of nurses working in that specialty.

A typical **special interest association** is the National Student Nurses Association. The main goal of this organization is to socialize the nursing students into the profession (Kittrell Chitty, 1997).

Two more broad purpose and well known professional organizations are the National League for Nurses and the State Board of Nursing.

The National League for Nurses

In the NLN nurses, other health professionals and consumers/clients work together to advance health care through nursing. The NLN strifes to assure quality nursing education and consequently quality health care through accreditation, continuing education programs, test services, research, publications, videos and lobbying efforts (see Kittrell Chitty, 1997).

The main and basic instrument to achive quality nursing education is the NLN's accreditation process for nursing education programs (see chapter 7, Quality Nursing Education). Accreditation is granted by the organization when educational programs comply with the numerous structural, curricular and outcome criteria (see Buckley Viertel, 2001). The accreditation process is applied to nursing education programs nationwide and therefore a certain national level of quality nursing education can be achieved.

The State Board of Nursing

State Boards of Nursing exist in every State of the United States. The overall organization of the State Boards is the National Council of State Boards of Nursing. The main reason for the existence of State Boards of Nursing is their responsibility to ensure quality nursing care for patients (see chapter 4, State Board of Nursing). In order to fulfil this responsibility State Boards have a legal mandate to establish certain professional rules and regulations for nursing.
This means State Boards determine and monitor the education of nurses. They approve on the basis of certain criteria the opening, running and periodic re-certification of nursing schools. They specify the qualifications of teachers at nursing schools.

specialty practice – fachspezifische Pflegepraxis, **to recruit** – anheuern, **main goal** – Hauptziel, **to strife for** – danach streben, **accreditation** – Anerkennung/Akkreditierung, **to achieve** – erreichen, **to grant** – gewähren, **to comply** – erfüllen, **nationwide** – in allen Bundesstaaten, **State Boards of Nursing** – Pflegekammer, **overall organization** – Dachorganisation, **responsibility** – Verantwortung, **to fulfil** – erfüllen, **legal mandate** – gesetzlicher Auftrag, **rules and regulations** – Regeln und Anordnungen, **mean** – bedeuten, **determine** – festlegen, **to monitor** – überwachen, **running** – Durchführung, **re-certification** – erneute Zertifizierung

The educational section of State Boards sets up the content and time frame of the so called State Board Examinations. Nurses who successfully pass the examination are licenced to practice professional nursing. They are also admitted to the register/list of registered nurses or licenced practical nurses and thus become RNs or LPNs. This way all professional nurses are registered with the Board.
This organization requires of each nurse the annual fulfilment of a certain number of hours of postgraduate education in order to renew the individual licences for professional practice.

On account of their legal mandate they can execute disciplinary action in cases of professional misconduct of their members.

Aside of the fulfilment of their responsibility for quality nursing care through the above means, State Boards of Nursing work closely with other professional organizations such as universities, hospitals, state organizations, unions and the ministries of health (for a detailed description of State Boards see Kellnhauser E. 1993).

content – Inhalt, **time frame** – zeitlicher Rahmen, **State Board Examination** – Staatsexamen, **to licence** – lizenzieren, **to register** – einschreiben, **annual fulfilment** – jährliche Erfüllung, **postgraduate** – nach Grundausbildung, **to renew** – erneuern, **on account** – basierend auf, **to execute** – durchführen, **disciplinary action** – Disziplinärmaßnahmen, **misconduct** – Fehlverhalten, **unions** – Gewerkschaften

Experiences with professional internships in the United States

During their studies of Pflegepädagogik und Pflegemanagement an der Katholischen Fachhochschule in Mainz the students are encouraged to do an internship in a foreign country. During the first seven years of the existence of these study courses 26 % of the students did spent time abroad. The majority of them did internships in the United States. Following are two students' accounts of their experiences during this time.

Hospitation am Alexian Brothers Medical Center, Elk Grove Village, Illinois

(Regina Assel)

1. Die Praktikumidee

Die Idee, ein Praktikum im Ausland zu machen, wurde durch den Pflegestudiengang an der Katholischen Fachhochschule in Mainz initiiert und gefördert. Die Pflege in Deutschland ist durch den Vorsprung der Professionalisierung der Pflege der »großen Schwester« USA stark beeinflusst. Dies wurde für mich als Pflegestudentin u.a. daran deutlich, dass große Teile pflegewissenschaftlicher Literatur Übersetzungen aus dem Amerikanischen und Englischen sind und dass Systeme aus diesem Sprachraum wie zum Beispiel Primary nursing, Casemanagement und Clinical Pathways, in Deutschland Einzug halten. Dies bedeutete für mich auch, dass Pflegende Qualifikationen brauchen, um sich mit den Gegebenheiten anderer Gesundheitssysteme auseinander zu setzen. Eine Möglichkeit, sich dem zu nähern, sah ich für mich in der Aufbesserung der fachsprachlichen Kenntnisse und in einem Besuch einer Gesundheitseinrichtung in den USA.
Nun musste nur noch eine Einrichtung gefunden werden, in der das Praktikum stattfinden konnte. Meine Studienrichtung Pflegepädagogik lässt vielleicht erwarten, dass vor allem eine Ausbildungseinrichtung in Frage kommt. Jedoch interessierten mich vor allem die Anforderungen der Pflegepraxis, auf die die Auszubildenden vorbereitet werden müssen. Also wählte ich für das Praktikum ein Krankenhaus. Der Kontakt zum Praktikumsort kam über einen Mitstudenten eines höheren Semesters und über Frau Prof. Dr. Kellnhauser zustande, die mich bei der Korrespondenz tatkräftig unterstütze. Mit wenigen organisatorischen Abstimmungen mit der »Vicepresident of Nursing« konnte das Praktikum in der Zeit vom 3. bis 29.08.1997 stattfinden.

2. Das Alexian Brothers Medical Center

Das Alexian Brothers Medical Center (ABMC) befindet sich in einer der westlichen Vororte von Chicago, in Elk Grove Village, nahe der grünen Lunge von Chicago, dem Forest Preserve, und ca. zwanzig Autominuten vom internationalen Flughafen O`Hare entfernt.

account – Aufzeichnung, **experience** – Erfahrung

Seit 130 Jahren folgen die Alexian Brothers ihrer Mission, für die physischen, emotionalen und spirituellen Bedürfnisse der Gemeinde zu sorgen. 1865 kamen die Brüder, deren Mutterhaus in Aachen ist, in die Vereinigten Staaten. Dort gründeten sie neben Elk Grove in St. Louis (Missouri), San Jose (California), Signal Mountain (Tennessee) und Milwaukee (Wisconsin) verschiedene Einrichtungen.
Das ABMC ist für 470 Betten zugelassen. Etwa 40 medizinische Fachrichtungen sind auf den zehn Pflegestationen vertreten. Zum ABMC gehören außer dem Akutkrankenhaus ein Rehabilitationszentrum, ein Zentrum für Psychiatrie und eine Gemeindepflegestation.

3. Die Gestaltung des Praktikums

Während meines Aufenthaltes war ich der Leiterin der innerbetrieblichen Fort- und Weiterbildung zugeordnet, die meine Ansprechpartnerin während des gesamten Aufenthalts war. Die Gestaltung des Programms ergab sich aus meinen Interessen, die schwerpunktmäßig im Bereich Aus-, Fort- und Weiterbildung und im Kennenlernen von professioneller Pflege und Gesundheitssystem in den Vereinigten Staaten lagen. Vor diesem Hintergrund wurde es mir ermöglicht, eine Reihe von Personen aus verschiedenen Abteilungen kennen zu lernen, sie zu befragen und an mehreren Konferenzen teilzunehmen.
In der verbleibenden Zeit hatte ich Gelegenheit zum Studium von Literatur aus der Krankenhausbibliothek, die neben einer großen Auswahl an Material zum Pflegeprozess und Pflegeliteratur zu den medizinischen Fachgebieten allein 16 verschiedene Pflegefachzeitschriften anbietet. Die folgende Auflistung gibt einen Überblick über die Praktikumsinhalte.

Programm

Personalentwicklung
- Teilnahme an den monatlich stattfindenden Einführungstagen für neue Mitarbeiter,
- Kennenlernen der innerbetrieblichen Fort- und Weiterbildung, Informationsgespräche mit der Leiterin der Abteilung.

Ausbildung
- Besuch des Harper Colleges, Teilnahme an einer Vorlesung,
- Besuch der St. Xaviers University, Gespräch mit der Direktorin des Bachelor-Studiengangs, Teilnahme an einer Vorlesung, Besichtigung des Skillslabs,
- Begleitung der Pflegepraxisanleiterin des Harper Colleges bei Lernbegleitungen von Studentinnen in der Praxis, Gelegenheit zum Austausch mit den Studentinnen.

Qualitätssicherung
- Kennenlernen der Abteilung Qualitätssicherung im ABMC, Informationsgespräche mit der Qualitätskoordinatorin und dem Direktor der Abteilung, kennen lernen der Rolle der Joint Commission im externen Qualitätsvergleich der Gesundheitseinrichtungen,
- Hospitation der monatlichen Konferenz des Komitees für klinische Praxis: In dieser Konferenz werden stationsübergreifende Fragen und Probleme aus der Praxis besprochen und bearbeitet,
- Hospitation an einer Konferenz zur Qualitätssicherung der pädiatrischen Klinik, an der die Behandlungsfälle der vergangenen drei Monate evaluiert werden.

Management
Kennenlernen des großen Aufgabenspektrums der Stationsleitung, speziell Personal- und Finanzverantwortung.

Gremien
- Hospitation interdisziplinärer Pflegevisiten,
- Begleitung einer Intensivfachpflegekraft zur Committee-Conference der Association of Critical Care Nurses – Illinois, Einblick in die Arbeit des Fachverbandes,
- Hospitation einer Ethikkonferenz, in der nach einem intensiven Entscheidungsfindungsprozess die Entscheidung in einem aktuellen Fall getroffen werden konnte.

Handlungsfelder
- Hospitation im Handlungsfeld Intensivstation; Kennenlernen der Aufgaben von Intensivfachpflegekräften auf der Intensivstation, Kennenlernen der Rolle und Aufgabe von Clinical Specialists im Praxisfeld,
- Kennenlernen des Beschwerdemanagements, Informationsgespräch mit der zuständigen Patient Representative,
- Kennenlernen klinischer Behandlungspfade (Clinical Pathways) und des Aufgabengebietes von Casemanagern,
- Begleitung einer Nurse Practitioner und Kennenlernen ihres Aufgabengebietes in enger Kooperation mit einem Vertragsarzt der Klinik,
- Besichtigung der Operationsabteilung, Hospitation einer OP,
- Besichtigung der Entbindungsstation und der Neugeborenen-Intensivstation,
- Kennenlernen der häuslichen Pflege, eine Abteilung, die der Klinik angeschlossen ist, Begleitung einer Pflegeperson auf ihrer Tour.

4. Ausgewählte Schwerpunkte des Praktikums

Externe Qualitätssicherung in der innerbetriebliche Fortbildung

Die Innerbetriebliche Fortbildungsabteilung gliedert sich inhaltlich in zwei Schwerpunkte auf, die Einführung neuer Mitarbeiter und die laufende Fortbildung für das Pflegepersonal. Beide Bereiche unterliegen ausführlichen Vorschriften der *ANCC* (American Nurses Credentialing Center´s Commission on Accreditation), eine Organisation, die der American Nurses Association (ANA) untergeordnet ist und ein Programm zur Überprüfung und Akkreditierung von Fortbildungsveranstaltungen im Pflegebereich entwickelt hat. Ihr Ziel ist, die Kompetenz der Pflegekräfte orientiert an den aktuellen und zukünftigen Anforderungen an das Berufsfeld weiterzuentwickeln.
1974 gründete die ANA zum Zweck der Überprüfung und Akkreditierung ein Voluntärsystem, das aus Pflegekräften besteht, die anhand von Standards und Kriterien Fortbildungsaktivitäten beurteilen und genehmigen. Dieser Genehmigungsprozess findet in einer Einrichtung normalerweise alle 7 Jahre statt und betrifft außer allen Klinken auch sämtliche Aus- und Weiterbildungseinrichtungen.
Die Akkreditierung der ANCC stellt für eine Klinik die Zulassung dar, Ausbildung anbieten beziehungsweise durchführen zu dürfen. Dies ist wiederum ein entscheidender Gesichtspunkt im Akkreditierungsprozess durch die Joint Commission on Accreditation of Healthcare Organisations (JCAHO). Diese Kommission, die Aufgaben der externen Qualitätssicherung im gesamten Gesundheitswesen übernommen hat, akkreditiert eine Klinik nur

dann, wenn es eine akkreditierte innerbetriebliche Fortbildungsabteilung nachweisen kann. Die Ergebnisse einer Akkreditierung werden veröffentlicht. Sie werden damit zum Aushängeschild einer Klinik. Nicht akkreditiert bedeutet, dass die Kostenträger auch ihre Zahlungsbereitschaft zurückziehen.

Pflegeprozess in Ausbildung und Praxis

Pflegeprozess in der Ausbildung

Das Thema Pflegeprozess bewegt die Pflege und Pflegeausbildung auch heute immer wieder. Aus diesem Grund interessierte mich, was die USA dazu anzubieten haben. Nach den Vorgaben des Illinois Nursing Practice Act ist der Pflegeprozess mit den Schritten der Anamnese, Analyse und Diagnose, Planung, Implementierung und Evaluation ein zentraler Inhalt in der Pflegeausbildung. Am Harper College wird dazu unterstützend die Pflegetheorie von Neuman herangezogen. Das in diesem Konzept enthaltene Neuman Wheel dient dabei der Prioritätenfindung in den physiologischen, psychologischen, soziokulturellen, entwicklungsbedingten und spirituellen Bedürfnissen des Patienten. In die psychologische und soziokulturelle Anamnese fließt Eriksons Theorie der Entwicklung der Persönlichkeit ein, wonach der Patient seiner Entwicklungsstufe zugeordnet werden soll. Die Beschäftigung mit dem Pflegeprozess beginnt im ersten Ausbildungsjahr. Die Studierenden werden mit ausführlichen Anamneseformularen des Colleges vertraut gemacht und lernen anhand von fiktiven Beispielen den Umgang damit. Vertieft wird dies im Praxiseinsatz. Anhand der so erstellten Anamnesen werden mit Hilfe von den von der NANDA (North American Nursing Diagnosis Association) anerkannten Pflegediagnosen Pflegepläne erstellt, die beurteilt werden. Im zweiten Ausbildungsjahr werden die Pflegepläne mit ortsüblichen Anamnesebögen festgelegt. Inhaltlich sind die Pflegeplanungen im ersten Ausbildungsjahr mehr auf das gesunde Individuum und seine Bedürfnisse bezogen, im zweiten Jahr mehr krankheitsbezogen. Zur Übung werden Kurzpläne erstellt, in denen die Studierenden sich auf die beispielsweise fünf wichtigsten Pflegediagnosen beschränken sollen.

Pflegeprozess in der Praxis

Im ABMC hat ein Team von Pflegekräften Standardpflegepläne entwickelt, die sich auf die dort am häufigsten vorkommenden medizinischen Diagnosen beziehen. In den einzelnen Plänen sind die bei der bestimmten Diagnose auftretenden Pflegediagnosen und die entsprechenden Maßnahmen aufgelistet. Es handelt sich also um Basisstandards, in denen individuelle Gesichtspunkte des speziellen Patienten nicht berücksichtigt sind. Diese können dann auf einem dazugehörigen Blatt ergänzt werden. Pläne für kombinierte medizinische Diagnosen gibt es nicht, entscheidend ist die Einweisungsdiagnose oder die im Vordergrund stehende Diagnose. Bei der Einweisung eines Patienten wird der entsprechende Pflegeplan aus dem Computer ausgedruckt und in die Akte geheftet. Selten wird der Plan mit individuellen Aspekten ergänzt. Mehr Wert misst man der Anamnese bei, die sehr ausführlich durchgeführt wird. Darin eingeschlossen ist unter anderem auch die körperliche Untersuchung. Diese wird täglich einmal pro Schicht durchgeführt und dokumentiert. Gerade die neuexaminierten Pflegekräfte sind über die Handhabung der Pflegeplanung in der Praxis überrascht, meist positiv, da für viele die Praktikabilität des in der Ausbildung vermittelten Umgangs mit dem Pflegeprozess fragwürdig gewesen ist. Die Verwendung von Standardpflegeplänen bietet somit eine Erleichterung in der Praxis.

Praxisanleitung in der Klinik
Durch die Begleitung von Frau Sterret, die Pflegepraxisanleiterin von Harper College, gewann ich einen Einblick in die Gestaltung der Praxiseinsätze. Sie begleitete eine Gruppe von acht Studentinnen, die auf den Stationen des ABMC eingesetzt waren. Jede war einer examinierten Pflegekraft zugeordnet, die der Studentin zwei bis drei ihrer Patienten/innen »übergab«. Die Studentinnen waren nahezu am Ende ihres ersten Ausbildungsjahres und wollten demnächst die Prüfung zur Licensed Practical Nurse ablegen. Inhaltlich stand die Gabe von Medikamenten, das Anhängen von Infusionen, die subkutane und intramuskuläre Injektion im Vordergrund. Da dies den Studentinnen eigenverantwortlich noch nicht erlaubt war, begleitete und überwachte die Praxisanleiterin jede dieser Tätigkeiten. Sie schätzte auch den Lernbedarf jeder einzelnen Studentin ein, um Lücken schließen oder Unsicherheiten nehmen zu können.
Die Studierenden lernen während ihrer Ausbildung verschiedene Krankenhäuser kennen, da die Praxisanteile nicht alle im gleichen Krankenhaus stattfinden. Der Einsatz in der häuslichen Pflege dauert meist nur zwei Tage.

Praxiserfahrung neben der Ausbildung
Neben der Ausbildung sammeln viele Studierende praktische Erfahrungen, indem sie nebenbei als Nursing Assistant (entspricht der Schwesternhelferin) oder als Nurse Intern (diese Person hat keinen Schwesternhelferinnenkurs, man rechnet ihr an, dass sie sich zur Zeit in Ausbildung befindet) arbeitet. Einige arbeiten auch als Stationssekretärin und haben so den Zugang zur Krankenpflege gefunden. Auf diese Art haben die meisten vor Beginn der Ausbildung Kontakt mit dem Gesundheitswesen gehabt, was ihnen den Einstieg und die Zeit nach der Ausbildung erleichtert.

5. Evaluation

Ein Auslandspraktikum bietet einen reichen Schatz an Erfahrungen für die weitere Karriere. Die Alexian Brothers boten mir diese Möglichkeit, wofür ich ihnen sehr dankbar bin. Überraschend war vor allem die Offenheit, mit der man mir als Praktikantin begegnete und die Bereitschaft, sich über verschiedene Systeme auszutauschen und diese kritisch zu beleuchten. Verschlossene Türen gab es nicht, auch nicht in kritischen Situationen, die beispielsweise ein Gremientreffen bieten kann, all dies wurde so zu einem spannenden Lernfeld.
Mir ist bei diesem Besuch bewusst geworden, wie wichtig es ist, sich auch international auszutauschen, um voneinander zu lernen und um sich gegenseitig unterstützen zu können.

6. Persönliche Erfahrungen

Umrahmt wurde der Aufenthalt am Rande Chicagos durch Besuche dieser großen Stadt am Lake Michigan, in der die Route 66 beginnt. Hier gibt es nicht nur viel Jazz, sondern auch Theater, Musicals und Festivals. Daneben ließen mich die engagierten Nurses des ABMC auch an ihrem Alltag und zu Hause teilhaben. So ergaben sich Einladungen zu einer Teamfeier anlässlich eines Masterabschlusses einer Kollegin und weitere gemeinsame Abendaktivitäten. Das forderte nicht nur vertiefte alltagssprachliche Kenntnisse, sondern ließ den Aufenthalt auch zu einem wertvollen persönlichen Erlebnis werden.

Hospitation in den Home Health Services des St. John's Hospital in Springfield, Illinois

(Monika Kotik)

Motivation für meine Hospitation

Während meines Studiums des Pflegemanagements an der Katholischen Fachhochschule in Mainz von 1997–2001 bin ich auf die Möglichkeit eines Auslandspraktikums in den USA aufmerksam geworden. Gewisse Aussagen von Frau Prof. Dr. Kellnhauser, unserer Professorin in Pflege, haben mich auf die Pflege in den USA neugierig gemacht. Speziell hat mich die Umsetzung bestimmter Instrumente, die für mich neu und theoretisch waren, in den pflegerischen Alltag interessiert.

Ich entschied mich für eine Hospitation in der ambulanten Pflege. So absolvierte ich mein Praktikum bei den Home Health Services des St. John's Hospital in Springfield/Illinois. Außerdem hospitierte ich einen Tag im St. John's Hospital, einenTag im angegliederten Hospiz und zwei Tage in einem städtischen Altenheim.
In diesem Beitrag möchte ausschließlich über meine Erfahrungen in den Home Health Services (HHS) berichten, da ich hier den größten Einblick gewann.

Meine Vorbereitung

Im Hinblick auf meine sprachliche Vorbereitung besuchte ich die von Frau Prof. Dr. Kellnhauser duchgeführte Vorlesungsreihe »Englische Fachterminologie«. In diesen Vorlesungen wurde nur englisch gesprochen und englische Fachliteratur behandelt, um die entsprechenden Pflegefachausdrücke kennenzulernen.
Außerdem bestand jede Vorlesung aus Rollenspielen, in denen alltägliche Szenen von Pflegenden in englischer Sprache nachgespielt wurden.
Meine Vorbildung bestand nur aus dem Schulenglisch bis zum Abitur. Die Sprache zu verstehen fiel mir nicht schwer, aber in den Rollenspielen fachlich richtig zu antworten, bereitete mir Probleme. Mit der Zeit wurde ich jedoch immer sicherer.
Zuhause schaute ich mir manchmal im Fernsehen beim Sender CNN die Nachrichten an, um mit der Sprache vertrauter zu werden.
Die Beschäftigung mit englischer Fachliteratur kann ich nur empfehlen, denn sie war für mich sehr hilfreich.

Bei der Praktikumplatzsuche half mir ein Kommilitone, der mir die Adresse vom St. John's Hospital in Springfield gab.
Der Pflegedirektor des Krankenhauses stellte den Kontakt zur ambulanten Pflege her, die mir auch unkompliziert die Zusage für den Zeitpunkt und die Dauer meines Praktikums gab.
Da ich als Studentin »knapp bei Kasse« war, organisierte die Pflegedirektorin der ambulanten Pflege eine private Unterkunft bei Virginia, einer hospice nurse.
Ich hatte bei ihr 4 Wochen freie Kost und Logis.

Die Home Health Services (HHS) des St. John's Hospital in Springfield/Illinois

Im Nachstehenden berichte ich über das Wesen, die einzelnen Leistungsbereiche und über die Pflegeorganisation der HHS. Aufgrund meiner deutschen Ausbildung als Altenpflegerin war es mir in den USA nicht erlaubt, in der Pflege mitzuarbeiten. Daher stand ich bei den Verrichtungen dabei, habe zugeschaut und zugehört.

1. Vorstellung der Home Health Services (HHS)

Die HHS gibt es seit 1984.
Ihr Ursprung liegt jedoch ca. 120 Jahre zurück. Damals kamen Schwestern des Franziskanerordens aus Deutschland nach Springfield und halfen dort den alten, kranken, armen und hungernden Menschen mit Essen, Medikamenten und ihrer Glaubensüberzeugung. Zu Fuß oder wenn eine Familie, die Hilfe bedurfte, sehr weit außerhalb der Stadt wohnte, auch mit dem Pferdewagen, brachten sie die benötigten Dinge. Diese Tradition bildet die Grundlage für die Philosophie der Pflege der HHS heute.

Die ambulante Pflege beschäftigte 1998 ca. 150 Mitarbeiter in Voll- und Teilzeit in Springfield und in der Außenstelle Decatur, die seit einem Jahr bestand.
Die Mitarbeiter gehören verschiedenen Berufsgruppen an: RNs, LPNs, und CNAs, Sekretärinnen, Physiotherapeuten, Logotherapeuten, Sozialarbeiter, Arbeiterinnen, Reinigungspersonal, Fahrer …

Die HHS gehören zum St. John's Hospital, und werden als Profit-Center betrieben. Deren Pflegedirektorin, Ann, ist deshalb nicht dem Pflegedirektor des Krankenhauses unterstellt, sondern dem Verwaltungsdirektor.
Sie sagte mir, dass ihr das so auch lieber wäre. Personal könnte bei Engpässen nicht von der ambulanten Pflege abgezogen und im Krankenhaus eingesetzt werden und umgekehrt.
Der Einsatzbereich umfasst Springfield und Umgebung sowie die Außenstelle in Decatur.

Sehr viele Schwestern haben neben ihrer Berufsausbildung eine zusätzliche Spezialisierung in Bezug auf ein Krankheitsbild oder eine Behandlungsmethode (z.B. Diät, Bewegungsübungen, Infusionstherapie, Bedienung von med. Maschinen, Herzerkrankungen, Umgang mit Sterbenden …)

2. Leistungsbereiche des HHS

Home Health Services ist in 6 Leistungsbereiche gegliedert, die jeweils von einem Supervisor (im deutschen vergleichbar mit einer Bereichsleitung) mit Masterabschluss geleitet werden. Dies sind:

2.1 Nursing Services

Im Vordergrund der Behandlung durch die HHS steht der Patient.
Eine RN macht den Erstbesuch bei einem Patient und erhebt dessen Wünsche und Hilfebedarf und wird dadurch seine »primary nurse«. Aufgrund ihres »care plan« werden Pflegemitarbeiter unterschiedlichster Qualifikation und andere Leistungserbringer der HHS wie z.B. Sozialarbeiter, Physiotherapeuten oder Logopäden tätig.
Sie ist die Person, die für jede Art von Hilfe durch HHS für den Patienten letztendlich verantwortlich ist. Bei ihr laufen alle Fäden zusammen.

Pflegemitarbeiter werden entsprechend ihrer Qualifikation eingesetzt. So kann es sein, dass an einem Tag 2-3 Mitarbeiter der HHS bei einem Patienten tätig werden.
Die CNAs (Pflegehelferinnen) werden für die Grundpflege eingesetzt, die LPNs für die Grund- und Behandlungspflege und die RNs zur Koordination und Überwachung der pflegerischen Versorgung des Patienten, sowie für die anspruchsvolle Behandlungspflege. Darunter fallen Tätigkeiten wie: Blut abnehmen, Lunge abhören, das Abhören der Herzfrequenz und der Darmgeräusche.
Jeder erfüllt hier ganz selbstverständlich seinen Part an der Pflege und Betreuung des Patienten, entsprechend seiner Qualifikation.
Diese professionelle Einstellung hat mir gefallen. Ich hatte nicht den Eindruck, dass die CNAs das Gefühl haben, minderwertigere Arbeit zu verrichten als die LPNs oder RNs.
In den USA arbeitet man schon länger mit den DRGs. Auch dort versucht man die Verweildauer der Patienten in den Krankenhäusern so niedrig wie möglich zu halten, was zur Konsequenz hat, dass die Patienten früher nach Hause entlassen werden, aber dort noch weitere Hilfe benötigen. Die HHS haben sich darauf eingestellt und bieten zu verschiedenen Krankheitsbildern spezielle Hilfeleistungen an (z. B. bei geriatrischen Erkrankungen, Herzerkrankungen, Krebserkrankungen usw.). Die Mitarbeiter müssen Zusatzqualifikationen erwerben, damit die HHS überhaupt in diesen spezialisierten Bereichen tätig werden können.
Es gibt auch intake/referral Nurses, die Patienten des St. John´s Hospital, die dort in Kürze entlassen werden – und weiter Hilfe brauchen –, die Dienste der ambulanten Pflegeeinrichtung anbieten. Möchten die Patienten die Hilfe in Anspruch nehmen, sorgen sie für eine reibungslose Überleitung der pflegerischen Versorgung zu der »primary nurse«. So ist eine kontinuierliche und weiterführende Betreuung und Behandlung des Patienten möglich.
Die Kosten für Dienste der HHS werden von den Versicherungen bei den einzelnen Erkrankungen für einen festgelegten Zeitraum übernommen. Dauert die Inanspruchnahme der Nursing Services länger, muss die »primary nurse« dies umfassend begründen und nachweisen können (care plan!), sonst stellt die Versicherung die Bezahlung ein.
Die Mitarbeiter der Nursing Services sind in Voll- oder Teilzeit beschäftigt.

2.2 Hospice/Psych./HHS Clinical Services

Für diese Bereiche haben die darin tätigen Registered Nurses spezielle Zusatzausbildungen bzw. haben ihr Master Degree in Hospiz-Pflege, Psychologie u. a.

2.3 Home Infusion & Perinatal Services

Damit HHS in diesen beiden Leistungsbereichen tätig werden kann, müssen die Patienten bestimmte Erkrankungskriterien erfüllen/Behandlungserfordernisse aufweisen, damit die Versicherungen die Kosten für einen festgelegten Zeitraum übernehmen.
Die Mitarbeiter – alle mit Zusatzqualifikation für ihren speziellen Bereich – sind hier in Voll- und Teilzeit beschäftigt.

2.4 Private Care Connection Program

In diesem Leistungsbereich werden angeboten: Verbandswechsel, Körperpflege, Mahlzeitenzubereitung, Hausputz, Einkaufen, Fahrten zum Arzt, zur Krankenkasse, Besorgungen erledigen, Vorlesen, Betreuen, Dasein.

Die Inanspruchnahme der Schwester für private care muss mindestens 3 Stunden betragen, Höchstdauer 24 Std. am Stück. Eine Schwester, die im Haus eines Kunden ist, macht *alles*. Daher ist es wichtig vorher zu schauen, welches die qualifikationshöchste Tätigkeit ist, um auch die Schwester mit der entsprechenden Ausbildung hinzuschicken. So kann es sein, dass ein Kunde eine Schwester für einen Verbandswechsel und zum Hausputz möchte. Beide Tätigkeiten werden von *derselben* Schwester durchgeführt (Unterschied zu den Nursing Services!).
Die Kunden müssen für den Service des Private Care Connection Program selbst bezahlen. Keine Krankenkasse übernimmt die Kosten.
Hier steht nicht die aktivierende, auf Selbstständigkeit und Unabhängigkeit bezogene Pflege im Vordergrund, sondern das Erbringen einer Dienstleistung. Daher spricht man in diesem Bereich eher vom Kunden als vom Patienten.

Alle Mitarbeiter sind zu Hause und werden bei Bedarf angerufen. Sie arbeiten auf Abruf. Die Dienstplangestaltung geschieht so, dass jeder sagt, wann er wie in einem Monat arbeiten könnte. Gibt es zu diesem Zeitpunkt Arbeit, bekommt er sie zugeteilt, wenn nicht, kann er auch kein Geld verdienen (unterscheidet sich von allen anderen Leistungsbereichen).

2.5 Business Management

Die Mitarbeiter dieses Leistungsbereichs haben die Kosten und Erlöse im Auge und arbeiten auch den »nurses« zu. Sie erledigen den Schriftverkehr mit den Ärzten und Versicherungen und schreiben Abrechnungen an die Patienten. Hat ein Patient kein Geld, um seine Medikamente zu bezahlen, versuchen sie über Kirchen oder wohltätige Organisationen Geld zu bekommen, damit die Versorgung des Patienten gewährleistet werden kann.
Ihnen kommt noch eine wichtige Aufgabe zu: die Überprüfung der Dokumentation bei verstorbenen oder ausgeschiedenen Patienten. Sie prüfen, ob die »primary nurse« die richtige Pflegediagnose ausgewählt hat und ob alle an der Pflege und Betreuung Beteiligten die beschriebenen Leistungen auch erbracht haben, da sonst die Bezahlung durch die Versicherung gefährdet wäre. Gibt es Unstimmigkeiten in der Dokumentation, geht diese zur Überarbeitung an die »primary nurse« zurück.

2.6 Decatur Branch

Kleine eigenständige Außenstelle, ca. 45 Min. Fahrt von Springfield entfernt.

3. Ausgewählte Elemente des Pflegemanagement

3.1 Pflegeleitbild

Aus der uneigennützigen Hilfe der Franziskanerinnen aus dem vorletzten Jahrhundert, leitet das St. John's Hospital und so auch die HHS seine Philosophie ab, was auch überall im Alltag zu spüren war.
Viele Mitarbeiter hatten über ihrem Schreibtisch, in Augenhöhe, die kleine Broschüre »Our Roles for a Successful Organization« hängen. In dieser ist die Philosophie für den täglichen Umgang miteinander genau beschrieben. Der Umgang mit den Patienten war geprägt von Herzlichkeit, Hilfsbereitschaft und einer professionellen Haltung.

3.2 Auswahl neuer Mitarbeiter

Die RNs sollten nicht jünger als 30 Jahre sein (um eine gewisse Lebenserfahrung mitzubringen) und müssen mindestens 2 Jahren nach ihrer Ausbildung im Beruf gearbeitet haben. Neben einem Vorstellungsgespräch findet ein schriftlicher Eignungstest statt. In diesem werden verschiedene Situationen der häuslichen Pflege dargestellt und die Bewerber sollen beschreiben, wie sie handeln würden (z. B. Erstellen eines Pflegeplans, Erstellen einer Patientenaufnahme, Führen eines Beratungsgesprächs, Handeln in einer Notfallsituation …). Diesen Test wertet der Supervisor aus und lädt die Bewerber nochmals ein, von denen er den besten Gesamteindruck hatte, und entscheidet dann nach einem weiteren Gespräch, welchen er nimmt.

3.3 Einarbeitung neuer Mitarbeiter

Die Einarbeitungszeit beträgt 12 Wochen und wird von den Nurses der Innerbetrieblichen Fortbildung organisiert, begleitet und überwacht.
Falls sie Schulungen benötigen, können die »Neuen« es sagen, damit entsprechende Fortbildung durchgeführt werden kann. Es gibt verschiedene Übungsprogramme. Danach erwartet man situationsgerechtes Handeln von den neuen Mitarbeitern. Vor dem ersten, alleinverantwortlichen Hausbesuch des neuen Mitarbeiters überprüft der Supervisor in einer skill training unit (Übungslabor) dessen Fähigkeiten.

3.4 Einführungstage für neue Mitarbeiter

HHS
Einmal monatlich findet ein Einführungstag für die neuen Mitarbeiter statt, unabhängig von der Zahl der Neueinstellungen und deren Aufgabengebiet (Fahrer, RN, Reinigungskraft).
Als ich daran teilnahm, waren es 5 Mitarbeiter.
Inhalte waren: Leitbild, Qualitätssicherung, Sicherheitsbestimmungen bei den Hausbesuchen (z.B. Verhalten bei Autopanne, Verhalten bei Angriff durch Betrunkene usw.), Hygienevorschriften u.v.m. Jeder Supervisor stellte auch seinen Leistungsbereich vor.

St. John's Hospital
Einmal monatlich finden auch zwei Einführungstage für neue Mitarbeiter des St. John's Hospital statt. Die neuen Mitarbeiter der HHS nehmen auch daran teil.
Inhalte waren hier: Geschichte und Entstehung des St. John's Hospital und seiner Philosophie (Filmvorführung), die Erläuterung des Organigramms (mit Bildvorstellung durch einen Diaprojektor), Hygienemaßnahmen (Demonstration und Filmvorführung), Altersversorgung, Urlaubsregelung, Abfallbeseitigung, Rückenschule, Qualitätssicherung, Verhalten im Brandfall usw.
Auch bei diesen Einführungstagen stellten die einzelnen Mitglieder ihre Bereiche selber vor. Auffallend war, dass viele Bereiche, die nicht direkt mit Pflege zu tun haben, von RNs geleitet wurden. So z.B. der Bereich Recycling oder auch Infection Control. Beide Rednerinnen waren RNs und haben sich in ihrem Beruf auf diese Bereiche spezialisiert.
Ich fand die Einführungstage wichtig und informativ, da sie einen Einblick in die verschiedensten Bereiche geben und man auch gleich die Ansprechpartner kennenlernt. Außerdem erhält man einen groben Überblick darüber, was in dieser Einrichtung von einem selber erwartet wird.

3.5 Stellenbeschreibungen

Jeder Mitarbeiter hatte eine, seiner Stelle entsprechenden, Stellenbeschreibung.
Er bekommt sie bei der Einstellung ausgehändigt. Sie bildet die Grundlage für die jährlichen Bewertungsgespräche.
Die Stellenbeschreibungen werden alle zwei Jahre überarbeitet.

3.6 Jährliche Beurteilungsgespräche

Exemplarische Vorstellung einer Beurteilungsgrundlage für eine RN:
Jedes Jahr, an seinem Einstellungstag, findet die jährliche Überprüfung des Mitarbeiters durch seinen Vorgesetzten statt.

Sie besteht aus mehreren Teilen:

1. Beobachtung während eines Hausbesuches
   Ca. 2–3 Tage davor kündigt der Supervisor der RN an, dass er sie in den nächsten Tagen zu einem Hausbesuch begleiten wird.
   Er beobachtet die RN während des Hausbesuches und fragt den Patienten und die Angehörigen, ob sie mit der Pflege der RN zufrieden sind.
2. Auswerten von 6 Patientenakten
   Der Supervisor mischt sie, indem er ins Archiv geht und sich Patientenakten holt, die abgeschlossen sind, sowie auch aktuelle.
   Diese schaut er nach bestimmten Kriterien durch:
   - Erheben der Anamnese, Auswahl der Pflegediagnose, Erstellen des Pflegeplans,
   - Umsetzung des Pflegeplans, ständige Anpassung an die Veränderungen, Anleiten der Patienten und fortlaufender Bericht,
   - Persönliche Erscheinung
     • gepflegt, keine Jeans, keine Shorts oder Röcke, die das Knie nicht bedecken,
   - Beschwerdebriefe oder Belobigungen durch Patienten.

Die Kriterien, nach denen eine RN bewertet wird, sind für alle gleich. Sie sind festgelegt und in einem Beurteilungsbogen niedergeschrieben. Jeder Bereich hat seinen spezifischen Beurteilungsbogen.
Auch alle anderen Mitarbeiter der HHS werden 1x jährlich von ihren Vorgesetzten beurteilt. An eine gute Beurteilung ist auch eine Gehaltserhöhung geknüpft.
Ich habe ihnen erzählt, dass es bei uns in Deutschland noch die Ausnahme ist, dass Mitarbeiter von ihren Vorgesetzen beurteilt werden. Das konnten sie kaum nachvollziehen, ebenso wenig auch, dass bei uns die Alterszugehörigkeit die tarifliche Vergütung anhebt.

3.7 Pflegedokumentation

Ihr Arbeitsmittel war der Computer. Jedem Mitarbeiter in den HHS steht ein Laptop zur Verfügung. Diese sind alle miteinander vernetzt. So kann jeder Mitarbeiter sämtliche Informationen eines Patienten von allen an der Pflege Beteiligten einsehen.
Nach dem Erstellen der Pflegeanamnese durch die »primary nurse« schlägt der Computer eine Pflegediagnose vor. Danach wird der Pflegeplan erstellt, die in die Behandlung involvierten Berufsgruppen informiert und anschließend alles mit dem Patienten besprochen. Die Dokumentation des Hausbesuches erfolgt von allen Mitarbeitern danach im Büro, in dem *jeder* einen kleinen eigenen Schreibtisch hat. Es muss fortlaufend dokumentiert werden, bei

Veränderung muss der »care plan« verändert werden. Ob eine Behandlung abgeschlossen ist oder weitergeführt wird, entscheidet die »primay nurse«. Sie erstellt auch den Abschlussbericht und gibt dann die vollständige Patientenakte an den Leistungsbereich Business Management ab.

4. Meine privaten Erlebnisse während dieser Zeit

Ich hatte gleich zu Beginn meiner Reise in die USA große Probleme. Am Flughafen in Frankfurt/Main befragte mich ein Sicherheitsbeamter vor dem Eincheckschalter, wohin ich in den Staaten reise möchte und was ich dort mache. Ich erzählte es ihm und er wollte von mir die Einladung der HHS sehen. Ich hatte sie nicht dabei. Er wollte auch die Adresse wissen, wo ich dort wohnen werde. Ich konnte sie ihm nicht sagen, da ich es selbst noch nicht wusste. Zeitweise war es ungewiss, ob ich überhaupt fliegen würde. Der Sicherheitsbeamte beriet sich mit seinem Vorgesetzten, der mich dann auch noch einmal befragte und nach 1 Std. Hin und Her konnte ich dann letztendlich einchecken. Daher mein Tipp: Nehmen Sie Einladungen oder sonstige Unterlagen mit, die Ihren Aufenthalt dort bestätigen.

Ich habe bei Virginia und Harry gewohnt. Ihr schönes Einfamilienhaus liegt außerhalb von Springfield. Mein Zimmer war riesig und ich hatte ein eigenes Bad und Toilette. Es gab im ganzen Haus keine Tür, die zu gewesen wäre oder gar abgeschlossen. Dieses Vertrauen in mich, einen für sie fremden Menschen, hat mich berührt.

Zuhause in Deutschland hatte ich mir überlegt, was ich den Leuten, bei denen ich wohnen werde, mitbringen könnte. Nach Rücksprache mit meiner Professorin, Frau Kellnhauser, besorgte ich eine Kuckucksuhr (ich stamme vom Fuße des Schwarzwaldes).
An meinem Ankunftstag saß ich abends mit Virginia und Harry beim Essen, als auf einmal ein »kuckuck, kuckuck« aus dem Wohnzimmer ertönte. Ich konnte es kaum fassen, aber da hing eine Kuckucksuhr! Ich musste lachen, ging in mein Zimmer und holte mein Geschenk für sie. Sie stimmten in mein Lachen ein, doch Harry hat noch am selben Abend einen Platz für mein Gastgeschenk gefunden.

Am ersten Wochenende nach meiner Ankunft wurde ich von den beiden in das Fox Theatre in St. Louis/Missouri eingeladen. Dort wurde das Musical »The Phantom of the Opera« aufgeführt. Es war beeindruckend. Dieses schöne alte Gebäude, das früher das Rathaus gewesen war, die Kulisse – es war phantastisch.

Auch das 2. Wochenende verbrachte ich im Bundesstaat Missouri. Ann, die Pflegedirektorin der HHS, hatte mich eingeladen. Es war ein großes Familienfest, an dem all ihre Geschwister (7 und deren Familie) sowie Verwandte teilnahmen. Wir wohnten in einem Hotel (das sie bezahlte), da ihre Mutter nicht alle Personen im Haus unterbringen konnte. Höhepunkt des Festes war ein Picknick in einem Park, zu dem jeder etwas zu essen und zu trinken mitbrachte. Virginia wollte für mich Cookies backen, die ich dann mitnehmen konnte. Das wollte ich nicht. So ging ich donnerstags mit Harry einkaufen, um verschiedene Käsesorten für eine Käseplatte zu kaufen. Der Käse war sehr teuer. Beim Picknick wurde von meiner Käseplatte kaum etwas genommen. Mir war dann auch klar warum nicht: Bei ihnen ist es nicht Tradition Käsehäppchen zu essen. Sie kannten es nicht und konnten so auch mit meinem Käse nichts anfangen.

Es war ein schönes und kurzweiliges Wochenende. Die Familienmitglieder bezogen mich in ihre Gespräche und Spiele mit ein, Jeff, Anns Mann, fuhr mit mir ein Stück des Mississippi entlang und wir besuchten den Heimatort von Mark Twain.

Virginia bat mich eines Abends mal was typisch Deutsches zu kochen. Ich schlug ihr Sauerbraten mit Nudeln vor. Sie war begeistert. Dies ist mir auch ganz gut gelungen. Problematischer war das Backen einer Schwarzwälder Kirschtorte. Geeignete Kirschen wie auch Speisestärke im Supermarkt zu finden gestaltete sich recht schwierig. Als »Speisestärkeersatz« nahm ich dann Maisstärke. Kirschwasser hatte ich aus Deutschland mitgebracht. Meine Torte sah schrecklich aus und schmeckte auch genauso. Gelernt habe ich daraus, dass man in einem anderen Land Dinge nicht gleich wie zu Hause machen kann und dass Stärke nicht gleich Stärke ist.

Die Mitarbeiter der HHS waren mir gegenüber sehr freundlich, offen und von teilweise großer Herzlichkeit. Ich bekam auf alle Fragen Antwort, konnte mir alle Unterlagen, die ich einsehen wollte, auch einsehen. Sie nahmen sich Zeit mir Dinge oder Abläufe zu erklären und waren sehr gastfreundlich.
Patrick, dem 4-jährigen Sohn meiner Freundin in Deutschland, hatte ich versprochen einen Indianerspeer mitzubringen. Ich habe mich so bemüht irgendwo einen zu kaufen, habe aber keinen bekommen. An meinem letzten Tag in den HHS lag Pfeil + Bogen, sowie ein Speer auf meinem Schreibtisch mit einem Brief von Hermie, einer CNA. Ich war gerührt. Auch ein Ansteck-Engel lag da, weil man (lt. Hermie) einen Schutzengel im Auto braucht und ich in meinem Auto in Deutschland keinen hatte.

5. Schlussbemerkungen

Ich könnte noch einige Beispiele mehr von Gastfreundschaft aufzählen, die ich erlebt habe, doch das sprengt diesen Rahmen. Das Praktikum war für mich eine persönliche wie fachliche Bereicherung. Noch heute stehe ich mit Virginia und Harry in losem Kontakt.
Ich habe eine patientenorientierte Pflege und Betreuung in den HHS kennengelernt. Viele Elemente der Aufbau- und Ablauforganisation, die ich bis dato nur theoretisch kannte, sah ich hier umgesetzt. Ebenso auch die Pflegeprozessmethode. Dies hilft mir heute beim Voranbringen der Strukturen in meinem Wirkungsbereich, wenn mich jemand bremsen will mit dem Argument »das geht doch gar nicht; das ist nicht leistbar oder umsetzbar«.
Ich glaube hier in Deutschland brauchen wir noch eine geraume Zeit, um zu der Entwicklung der Pflege in den USA aufschließen zu können. Doch wir haben uns auf den Weg gemacht und das war der wichtigste Schritt.

Zur besseren Lesbarkeit habe ich die männliche Anredeform gewählt. Der Inhalt ist jedoch auf beide Geschlechter bezogen.

Professional Nursing Journals

A selection of American Nursing Journals helpful in searching for a job:
American Journal of Critical Care
American Journal of Hospice and Palliative Care
American Journal of Nursing
American Nurse
ANNA Journal – American Nephrology Nurses' Association
AORN Journal – Association of Operating Room Nurses

Cancer Nursing
Critical Care Nurse
Critical Care Nursing Quarterly

Gastroenterology Nursing
Geriatric Nursing

Heart and Lung: The Journal of Acute and Critical Care
Home Healthcare Nurse

JANAC Journal of the Association of Nurses in AIDS Care
JEN Journal of Emergency Nursing
JOGNN Journal of Obstetric, Gynecologic, and Neonatal Nursing
Journal of Cardiovascular Nursing
Journal of Child and Adolescent Psychiatric Nursing
Journal of Community Health Nursing
Journal of Gerontological Nursing
Journal of Neuroscience Nursing
Journal of Nursing Education
Journal of Ophthalmic Nursing and Technology
Journal of Pediatirc Health Care
Journal of Pediatric Oncology Nursing
Journal of Vascular Nursing

Nursing 03
Nursing Management
Nursing Times

Oncology Nursing Forum
Orthopedic Nursing

Pediatric Nursing
Public Health Nursing

Rehabilitation Nursing
RN

Urologic Nursing

Helpful Addresses

Council Education USA
Amerikahaus
Staufenstrasse 1
60323 Frankfurt am Main
Telefon und Telefax (0 69) 97 20 56 49
Email ahf@councilexchanges.de
Website www.educationusa.de
Call Center: Telefonische Beratung, Mo.–Fr. von 10–18 Uhr

Commission on Graduates of Foreign Nursing Schools
3600 Market Street
Suite 400
Philadelphia, PA 19104-2651, USA
Telefon 001 (2 15) 349-8767
Telefax 001 (2 15) 349-0026
Website www.cgfns.org

National Council of State Boards of Nursing, Inc.
(Dachverband sämtlicher Pflegekammern)
676 North St. Claire Street, Suite 550
Chicago, Illinois 60611-2921
Phone 312-787-6555
Fax 312-787-6898
khellquist@ncsbn.org
Über diese Organisation können alle State Boards of Nursing erreicht werden.
Internet: http://ncsbn.org/files/boards/boardswebsites.asp

Sylvan Prometric
Zeil 5, 3. Stock
60313 Frankfurt am Main
Telefon (0 69) 13 37 41-0
Telefax (0 69) 13 37 41-10

Sylvan Prometric
Nymphenburgerstrasse 20a
80335 München
Telefon (0 89) 52 05 61-0
Telefax (0 89) 52 05 61-71

Sylvan Prometric
Neuerwall Strasse 34
20354 Hamburg
Telefon (0 40) 37 51 93 60
Telefax (0 40) 37 51 93 59

Sylvan Prometric
Torstrasse 49
10119 Berlin
Telefon (0 30) 44 02 38-51
Telefax (0 30) 44 02 51-59

Regional Registration Center for GED/TOEFL
CITO/Sylvan Learning Systems B.V.
Niewe Oeverstraat No. 50
6811 JB Arnhem
The Netherlands
Telefon 0031 (2 63 52) 15 77
Telefax 0031 (2 63 52) 12 78

Center for Communication in Health Care
Darmstädter Landstrasse 109
60598 Frankfurt am Main
Telefon (0 69) 61 87 53
Telefax (0 69) 61 87 56
Email Y.Ford@gmx.de

Website TOEFL
www. toefl. org

The address of the State Board of Nursing of each state of the United States can be obtained in the Internet: http://ncsbn.org/files/boards/boardswebsites.asp

Abbreviations in Nursing

Common national abbreviations in nursing relative to physicians' orders and/or treatments: Allgemein übliche, landesweit anerkannte Abkürzungen im Zusammenhang mit ärztlichen Verordnungen von Medikamenten und/oder Behandlungen:

	lateinisch	englisch	deutsch
a.c.	ante cibos	before meals	vor den Mahlzeiten
p.c.	post cibu	after meals	nach den Mahlzeiten
b.i.d.	bis in die	twice daily	2 x täglich – at 10am-6pm
t.i.d.	ter in die	three times daily	3 x täglich – at 10am-2pm-6pm
q.i.d.	quarter in die	four times daily	4 x täglich – at 10am-2pm-6pm-10pm
stat.	statim	immediately	sofort
p.r.n.	pro re nata	when necessary	wenn nötig
h.s.	hora somni	hour of sleep	vor dem Einschlafen
p.o.	per os	by mouth	oral
i.m.	intra musculus	intramuscularly	intramuskulär
s.c.	sub cutis	subcutaneously	subkutan
i.v.	intra vena	intravenously	intravenös
NPO	nil per os	nothing by mouth	Nahrungskarenz
i.e.	id est	that is	zum Beispiel
oz.	uncia	ounce	Unze, 30 ml.

DC – discontinue = stopp	(Arzneimittel/Behandlung)
DNR – Do Not Resuscitate	(keine Reanimation)
Diagnosis	singular
Diagnoses	plural

Literature

Alexian Brothers Medical Center, (1998) Good Connections: Telephone Communication Skills, Self-Study Programm. Chicago, Illinois

Apple, Kathy (2001) National Council of State Boards of Nursing, NCSBN Issues Position Paper on Foreign (International) Nurse Immigration. www.ncsbn.org

Barry University (2000/2001) Undergraduate Catalog. Miami, Florida

BlueCross BlueShield of Florida (2003) Blue Care for individuals under 65. Jacksonville, Florida, USA

BlueCross BlueShield of Florida (2003) Outline of Medicare Supplement Coverage, Jacksonville, Florida, USA

Buckley-Viertel, Dorotheee; (2001) Studieren und Pflegen in den USA. Huber, Bern

Cedars Medical Center (1997) Cedars Television Network. Miami, Florida

Cedars Medical Center (1998) Information for our Patients. Miami, Florida

Cedars Medical Center (1998) Nursing Orientation Manual. Miami, Florida

CGFNS – Commission on Graduates of Foreign Nursing Schools. Path to CGFNS Certification: Applicant Handbook. Edition 28, Philadelphia, PA. USA

Iglehart, John (1999) The American Health Care System – Medicaid. The New England Jourenal of Medicine, Volume 340, No. 5

Iglehart, John (1999) The American Health Care System – Medicare. The New England Journal of Medicine, Volume 340, No. 4

Joint Commission on Accreditation of Health Care Organizations (1991) An Introduction to Joint Commission Nursing Care Standards, Oakbrook Terrace, Ill. USA

Jonas, Steven; Kovner Anthony; (1999) Health Care Delivery in the United States. Springer, New York

Kellnhauser, Edith (1990) Die Position und Aufgabentellung des Nursing Supervisors in den USA. Die Schwester, Der Pfleger, Melsungen. Nr. 11

Kellnhauser, Edith (1991) Position und Aufgabenstellung einer Stationssekretärin. Erfahrungen aus den USA. Die Schwester, Der Pfleger, Melsungen Nr. 3

Kellnhauser, Edith (1991/1992) Ein Qualitätssicherungsprogramm für den Gesamtbetrieb Krankenhaus. Führen und Wirtschaften im Krankenhaus, Melsungen, 1991, Nr. 5, 6; 1992, Nr. 1

Kellnhauser, Edith (1993) Krankenpflegekammern und Professionalisierung der Pflege. Bibliomed, Melsungen

Kellnhauser, Edith (2000) Pflegeleitbild. in: Thiemes Pflege, Stuttgart, New York

Kittrel Chitty, Kay (1997) Professional Nursing – Concepts and Challenges. Second Edition. W.B. Saunders Company, Philadelphia

O'Bryan Doheny, Margaret; Cook, Christian Benson; Stopper, Mary Constance; (1997) The Discipline of Nursing. Fourth Edition. Appleton&Lange, Stamford, Connecticut, USA

Rowland, Howard, S.; Rowland, Beatrice,L., (1992) Nursing Administration Handbook. Aspen Publishers, Gaithersburg, Maryland

St. John's Hospital (2001) Employee Handbook. Springfield, Illinois

St. John's Hospital Department Manual (1998) Subject: Medical Moral Committee

St. John's Hospital (1995). Springfield, Illinois. Policy and Procedures.

St. John's Hospital, Position Description Director of Nursing, Springfield, Illinois

Index

a worst case scenario . . . . im schlimmsten Fall
abbreviated . . . . gekürzt
absence . . . . Abwesenheit
abuse. . . . . Missbrauch
acceptance. . . . . Annahme
accepted . . . . anerkannt
access . . . . Zugang/Verbindung
accidents. . . . . Unfälle
accommodations . . . . Unterbringung
accomplishment . . . . Erreichung
accordance . . . . Einklang
according . . . . entsprechend
accountability . . . . Beweisführung
accountable. . . . . nachweispflichtig
Accounting and Disbursement . . . . Buchhaltung und Ausgaben
accreditation manual. . . . . Zertifizierungshandbuch
accreditation . . . . Anerkennung
accredited . . . . anerkannt
accrediting and licencing agencies. . . . . Akkreditierungs- und Lizenzierungsbehörden
accrediting organization . . . . anerkennende Behörde
accrual . . . . Ansammlung
achievement . . . . Erreichung
acquisition . . . . Erwerb
act accordingly . . . . entsprechend handeln
action . . . . Maßnahme
actual hours worked . . . . tatsächlich gearbeitete Stunden
actual . . . . tatsächlich
adaptation. . . . . Anpassung
additional personal . . . . zusätzliches Personal
addressed in name. namentlich adressiert
adequate legal decision making mechanisms ausreichende rechtliche Entscheidungsmechanismen
administration . . . . Betriebsleitung/Vergabe
administrative leadership . . . . betriebliche Führung
administrative possibilities . . . . Managementmöglichkeiten
admission office . . . . Aufnahmebüro
admission . . . . Aufnahme
admitting and treatment privileges . . . . Aufnahme- und Behandlungserlaubnis
admitting nurse. . . . . Aufnahmeschwester
admitting privileges . . . . Aufnahme-Erlaubnis
adolescents . . . . Jugendliche
adult . . . . Erwachsener

advanced directives or living will. . . . . Patientenverfügung
advanced directives . . . . vorsorgliche Anweisungen
advancement. . . . . Aufstieg
advice . . . . Rat
advisable. . . . . ratsam
affection . . . . Verbundenheit
affiliated . . . . angeschlossen
affiliation . . . . Anschluss
agency. . . . . agentur
aggregates. . . . . Gruppen/Gemeinden
ahead of . . . . bevor
aims to accomplish . . . . angestrebt zu erzielen
aim . . . . Ziel
all circumstances. . . . . alle Umstände
allied professionals . . . . relevante Heilberufe
alongside. . . . . neben
alternations. . . . . Veränderungen
amount and intensity . . . . Arbeitsanfall und- intensität
amount of earnings. . . . . Summe des Verdienstes
annual budget. . . . . Jahresbudget
annual deductable. jährliche Selbstbeteiligung
annual fulfilment . . . . jährliche Erfüllung
annually . . . . jährlich
appearance . . . . Erscheinung
applicable to your conduct . . . . Ihr Verhalten betreffend
applicant. . . . . Antragsteller/Bewerber
application . . . . Antrag/Bewerbung/Anwendung
apply to all settings. . . . . bezogen auf alle Bereiche
appointments . . . . Termine
appropriate care . . . . entsprechende Pflege
appropriate conduct . . . . entsprechendes Verhalten
appropriate educational experience . . . . erforderliche Ausbildungserfahrung
appropriate hospital staff. . . . . entsprechende Krankenhausmitarbeiter
appropriate section . . . . entprechender Teil
appropriate . . . . angemessen/entsprechend
appropriateness. . . . . Angemessenheit/Entsprechung
approved amount . . . . bewilligte Summe
approved/comparable . . . . anerkannt/vergleichbar/bewilligt
approximate availability . . . . ungefähre Verfügbarkeit
are expected . . . . wird erwartet
area. . . . . Bereich, Gebiet
as a rule . . . . gewöhnlich
assets . . . . Besitz
assistance . . . . Unterstützung
assistant head nurse . . . . Stellvertretung der Stationsschwester
associate executive director . . . . stellvertretender Betriebsleiter
at all times . . . . immer
attendance . . . . Anwesenheit

attending physician . . . . behandelnder Arzt
attention paid . . . . Aufmerksamkeit widmen
attire . . . . Bekleidung
authorized . . . . beauftragt
auxiliary . . . . ehrenamtliche Hilfsdienste
availability of known financial ressources . . . Verfügbarkeit bekannter finanzieller Mittel
availability . . . . Verfügbarkeit
available . . . . vorhanden
award . . . . Auszeichnung

Bachelor Degree . . . . 1. Universitätsgrad
background knowledge . . . . Hintergrundwissen
base rate of pay . . . . Grundgehalt
based on . . . . aufbauend
basic rights of human beings . . . . menschliche Grundrechte
be aware . . . . wissen
beauticians and barber services . . . . Schönheits- und Friseurdienste
bed rails . . . . Bettgitter
bed sore prevention . . . . Dekubitusprophylaxe
bed sore . . . . Dekubitus
behavior . . . . Verhalten
belief . . . . Annahme/Einstellung/Auffassung
benefit programs . . . . Zusatzleistungsprogramme
benefits . . . . Nutzen/Zusatzleistungen
birthing centers . . . . Entbindungszentren
birthing . . . . Entbindung
blood pressure . . . . Blutdruck
board of directors . . . . Verwaltungsrat
board . . . . Aufsichtsrat
body of knowledge . . . . Wissensfundus
bomb threat . . . . Bombendrohung
breach of security . . . . Verletzung der Sicherheit
break . . . . pause
broad purpose . . . . breit angelegt
budget and cost . . . . Budget und Kosten
bulletin board . . . . Informationsbrett

capabilities . . . . Fähigkeiten
capable . . . . fähig
capitation . . . . Deckelung der Kostenerstattung
care . . . . Behandlung
career ladder . . . . Karriereleiter
caring behavior . . . . fürsorgliches Verhalten
caring climate . . . . fürsorgliche Atmosphäre
caring environment . . . . fürsorgliche Atmosphäre
carpet . . . . Teppich
case . . . . Fall
ceiling . . . . Zimmerdecke

CEO – chief executive officer . . . . Betriebsleiter
cerebral vascular accident . . . . Apoplexie
certain . . . . bestimmt
chairperson . . . . Vorsitzender
changing contingencies . . . . wechselnde Möglichkeiten
character . . . . Wesen
charge nurse . . . . stellvertretende Stationsschwester
charge position . . . . stellvertretend für Stationsschwester
charge . . . . Gebühr/Behandlungskosten
chart . . . . Plan
choice . . . . Auswahlmöglichkeit
circumstances . . . . Umstände
claimed violation . . . . angebliche Nichtbeachtung
clergy . . . . Geistliche
clinical and administrative records . . . . klinische und betriebliche Dokumentation
clinical ladder . . . . klinische Leiter
code . . . . Codex
collaborate . . . . mitarbeiten
collaboration . . . . Zusammenarbeit
colleague . . . . Kollegin
comfort . . . . Wohlergehen
commitment . . . . Verpflichtung
common abbreviations . . . . gewöhnlich angewandte Abkürzungen
common concern . . . . allgemeines Interesse
common educational basis . . . . einheitliche Wissensgrundlage
common . . . . gemeinsam
communicable diseases . . . . ansteckende Krankheiten
community at large . . . . Allgemeinheit
community health goals . . . . Gesundheitsziele der Gemeinde
community needs . . . . Bedürfnisse der Gemeinde
community . . . . Gemeinde
compassionate care . . . . einfühlsame Betreuung
compassion . . . . Mitleid/Empathie
competitive . . . . wettbewerblich
complaint . . . . Beschwerde
completion . . . . Abschluss
compliance . . . . mitmachen/Mitarbeit
composition . . . . Aufsatz
comprehensive health care . . . . umfassende Gesundheitsversorgung
conception . . . . Empfängnis
concerned . . . . befasst sein mit/besorgt sein
concern . . . . Sorge
concessions . . . . Zugeständnisse
concise explanation . . . . präzise Erklärung
condition . . . . Zustand
conducive . . . . fördernd
conduct . . . . Verhaltensweise
confidentiality . . . . Vertraulichkeit

confidential . . . . vertraulich
conformity . . . . Übereinstimmung
consecutive . . . . aufeinander folgend
consent forms . . . . Formulare zur Einwilligungserklärung
consent . . . . Einwilligung
considerable . . . . beachtlich
considerate . . . . fürsorglich
consideration . . . . Rücksichtnahme
constitutes official confirmation . . . . offizielle Bestätigung
consumer relations coordinator . . . . Koordinator der hausinternen Patientenanlaufstelle
consumer relations representative . . . . Leiter der hausinternen Patienten-anlaufstelle
consumer relations . . . . hausinterne Patientenanlaufstelle
consumer . . . . Verbraucher
contamination . . . . Verunreinigung
content . . . . Inhalt
continuing education . . . . Fortbildung
contracted . . . . vertraglich geregelt
contribution . . . . Beitrag
controlling agencies . . . . Kontrollbehörden
coordinators . . . . pflegerische Abteilungsleitungen
copayment . . . . Selbstbeteiligung
core benefits . . . . Kernzusatzleistungen
core values . . . . zentrale Werte
corporate administration . . . . Betriebsleitung
corrective Aktion . . . . korrektives Eingreifen
corresponding . . . . einhergehend
counseling . . . . Beratung
county . . . . Landkreis
couriers . . . . Hol- und Bringedienst
course . . . . Verlauf
courteous usage . . . . höfliche Bedienung
courteous . . . . höflich
coverage . . . . Abdeckung
covered services . . . . abgedeckte Behandlungen
crash cart . . . . Notfallwagen
creates a favorable impression . . . . bewirkt einen günstigen Eindruck
creation . . . . Errichtung
credit points applied . . . . gegebene Punktwerte
credit . . . . Anerkennung
creed . . . . Weltanschauung
crucial . . . . entscheidend
current professional licence . . . . gültige professionelle Berufserlaubnis
current regulations . . . . aktuelle Vorgaben
current . . . . aktuell
currently existing quality levels . . . . derzeit bestehendes Qualitätsniveau
currently . . . . derzeit

curtain . . . . Vorhang
customer satisfaction. Kundenzufriedenheit
customer. . . . . Kunde

danger. . . . . Gefahr
days off. . . . . freie Tage
debilitating . . . . invalidisierend
decision making process . . . . Entscheidungsfindungsprozess
decision making . . . . Entscheidung treffen
decisions which affect them . . . . Entscheidungen, die sie betreffen
decisions . . . . Entscheidungen
declaration of intent . . . . Festlegung einer Absicht
decreased public confidence . . . . Abnahme öffentlichen Vertrauens
deficiency . . . . Unzulänglichkeit
degree. . . . . Grad
dejected . . . . zurückgesetzt
delegate . . . . Vertreter
delivery of nursing care. . . . . Durchführung von Pflege
delivery. . . . . Entbindung
demand. . . . . Nachfrage
dentures . . . . Zahnprotesen
department head. . . . . Abteilungsleitung
department manual. Abteilungs-/Stationshandbuch
dependency. . . . . Abhängigkeit
depending. . . . . abhängig
designated. . . . . bestimmt/beauftragt
detection. . . . . Aufdeckung
determine . . . . festlegen
development and community relations . . . . . Entwicklung und Gemeindearbeit
development . . . . Entwicklung
devices . . . . Geräte
difficult. . . . . schwierig
dignity . . . . Würde
directed to . . . . ausgerichtet auf
directions . . . . Hinweise
directly related . . . . in direktem Zusammenhang
disability. . . . . Behinderung
disabled . . . . behindert
disappointed . . . . enttäuscht
disaster . . . . Katastrophe
discharge planing . . . . Entlassungsplanung
discharge. . . . . Entlassung
disciplinary action. . . . . Disziplinärmaßnahmen
discipline . . . . Fachbereich
disease . . . . Krankheit
disorders . . . . Erkrankungen
disrobed . . . . ausgezogen
dissatisfaction . . . . Unzufriedenheit

distress	Stress
diverse clientele	unterschiedliches Klientel
diversified	vielfältig
diversity	Vielfalt
division of nursing	der Pflegedienst
division	Abschnitt
doctor's office	ärztliche Praxis
domestic	einheimisch
dominant	vorherrschend
donations	Spenden
drapes	Vorhänge
drawer	Schublade
dress	Kleidung
drills	Übungen
drug	Medikament
due to	aufgrund von/infolge von
duely	gebührend
dues	Beiträge
durable medical equipment	haltbare medizinische Geräte
duration	Zeitraum
duty	Dienst
dysfunction	Bewältigungsunfähigkeit
easy access	leichten Zugriff
educational needs	Bildungsbedürfnisse
education	Bildung
effects	Auswirkungen
efforts	Anstrengungen
elections	Wahlen
electrical appliances	elektrische Geräte
elementary and secondary educational systems	Grundschule und höhere Bildungssysteme
eligible beneficiaries	berechtigte Nutzer
eligible	berechtigt
employable	einstellungsfähig
employed	angestellt
employee health and safety	Mitarbeitergesundheit und -sicherheit
employee of the month, the year	Mitarbeiter des Monats/des Jahres
employee performance	Leistung der Mitarbeiter
employer	Arbeitgeber
employment relationships	Anstellungsverhältnisse
employment	Anstellung
enhance	erhöhen
enrollment	Beitritt
entire	gesamt
entitled	berechtigt
entry	Eintritt
environmental hazard	Umweltgefahr

environment . . . . Umwelt
equality and continuity . . . . Gleichbehandlung und Kontinuität
equipment interference . . . . Funktionsstörung von Geräten
equipment. . . . . Geräte
equipped. . . . . ausgestattet
erroneous . . . . falsch
error . . . . Fehler
escort . . . . Begleitung
establishment . . . . Errichtung
ethical beliefs . . . . ethischen Eins
ethical issues . . . . ethische Aspekte
exact opposite . . . . genaue Gegenteil
examinations. . . . . Untersuchungen
exceeded . . . . überzogen
exception . . . . Ausnahme
excerpts. . . . . Auszüge
exchange. . . . . Austausch
execution . . . . Ausführung
executive director . . . . Betriebsleiter
executive vice president. . . . . stellvertretender Betriebsleiter
exercise . . . . Übung
existence of professional connection . . . . Bestehen professioneller Verbindung
expanded knowledge. . . . . erweitertes Fachwissen
expansion . . . . Erweiterung
expectation . . . . Erwartung
expenses . . . . Kosten
experience. . . . . Erfahrung
explanation . . . . Erklärung
extended. . . . . verlängert
extent permitted by law . . . . im gesetzlich erlaubten Ausmaß
extent . . . . Ausmaß

facility. . . . . Einrichtung
failure . . . . Nichtbestehen/Nichteinhalten
federal guidelines . . . . staatliche Richtlinien
federal. . . . . bundesstaatlich
fee for service . . . . Bezahlung für Leistung
fee schedule . . . . Bewilligungsraster
fellow patient . . . . Mitpatient
final outcome . . . . Endergebnis
finances. . . . . Finanzen
financial obligations . . . . finanzielle Verpflichtungen
floor nurses. . . . . Krankenschwestern auf Station
floors . . . . Pflegestationen
focus of attention . . . . Fokus des Geschehens
follow up care . . . . Nachsorge
foreign country. . . . . Ausland
foreign educated . . . . im Ausland ausgebildet

form	Formular
foundation	Grundlage
founding	Errichtung
framework	Rahmenkonzept
free of charge	kostenlos
freedom of expression	Meinungsfreiheit
frequency	Häufigkeit
frequent rounds	häufige Rundgänge
frequently	häufig
fund raising	Spendensammlung
funding	Finanzierung
furnishings	Mobiliar
furthermore	des Weiteren
general overview	allgemeiner Überblick
goal	Ziel
gospel	Evangelium
governing body	Verwaltungsrat
government funding	staatliche Gelder
governmental	staatlich
governments	Behörden
grade	note
graduate studies	Studien nach Erwerb des Bachelorgrades
grants	Zuwendungen
great first impressions	große erste Eindrücke
grievance	Beschwerde
group practice	Gruppenpraxis
guard chains	Sicherheitsketten
guardian	Vormund
guest tray	Besucheressen im Krankenzimmer
guidance	Führung
guideline	Leitfaden
guide	Richtschnur
handicap	Behinderung
handicapped	Behinderte
harrassment	Quälereien
health agency	Gesundheitsorganisation
health as wholeness	Gesundheit als Ganzheit
health care delivery effort	Gesundheitsversorgungsbemühen
health care delivery system	Gesundheitsversorgungssystem
health care education	Gesundheitserziehung
health care facilities	Gesundheitseinrichtungen
health care insurance	Krankenversicherung
health care providers	Gesundheitseinrichtungen
health care requirements	gesundheitliche Erfordernisse
health care services	Gesundheitsdienste
health facilities	Gesundheitseinrichtungen

health insurance carriers . . . . Krankenversicherungen
health issues . . . . gesundheitliche Aspekte
health personnel . . . . Gesundheitspersonal
health professional of the opposite sex . . . . . professionelle Person des anderen Geschlechts
highly-regarded . . . . hoch angesehen
hitherto. . . . . bislang
home health . . . . Häusliche Pflege
hopital policy . . . . Krankenhausrichtlinien
hospice movement . . . . Hospizbewegung
hospital administrator. . . . . Krankenhausbetriebswirt
hospital affiliated . . . . dem Krankenhaus angeschlossen
hospital premises . . . . Krankenhausgelände
hospital security . . . . krankenhauseigenes Sicherheits-/ Bewachungssystem
hospital staff. . . . . Krankenhausmitarbeiter
hospital stay . . . . Krankenhausaufenthalt
hospital supervisors. . . . . Abteilungsleiter/innen
hospitality. . . . . Gastfreundschaft
hospitalizations. . . . . Krankenhausaufenthalte
hotel accommodations . . . . Hotelunterkunft für Angehörige
house staff . . . . angestellte Ärzte
human relationships . . . . menschliche Beziehungen
human resources . . . . Personalabteilung

i. e. = id est . . . . zum Beispiel
identical level . . . . einheitliches Niveau
identification badge . . . . Identifikationskarte
identification bracelet . . . . Identifikations-Armband
illness . . . . Krankheit
image . . . . Eindruck
immediate. . . . . direkt
impartial access. . . . . unparteiischen Zugang
implications . . . . Auswirkungen
impression . . . . Eindruck
improvement . . . . Verbesserung
in a manner. . . . . in einer Art und Weise
in accordance . . . . im Einklang
in addition . . . . zusätzlich
in advance of treatment. . . . . vor der Behandlung
in advance. . . . . im vorhinein
in excess . . . . darüberliegend
in general . . . . im Allgemeinen
in good faith. . . . . vertrauensvoll
in keeping with. . . . . im Einklang mit
in particular . . . . speziell
in practice. . . . . wird durchgeführt
in terms . . . . durch einen Sprachgebrauch

in the interest	im Interesse
in the monetary sense	im geldlichen Sinn
in turn	wiederum
inability	Unfähigkeit
incident	Vorkommnis
increase	Zunahme
independent	selbstständig
in-depth relationship	vertieftes Verhältnis
indigent	mittellos
infection control measures	Hygienemaßnahmen
influx	Zustrom
informed judgement	wissensbasierte Entscheidung
in-house education	innerbetriebliche Fortbildung
initiation	Einleitung
injury	Verletzung
inscription	Inschrift
inservice education department	Innerbetriebliche Fortbildungsabteilung
inservice education	Innerbetriebliche Fortbildung
inservice teaching	innerbetriebliche Fortbildung
insignia	Abzeichen
installations	Einrichtungen
instructions	Anweisungen
insurance claims	Versicherungsansprüche
insurance	Versicherung
intake and output	Flüssigkeitsbilanz
integral part	wesentlicher Teil
intended destination	beabsichtigtes Ziel
interdepartmental relations	Beziehungen zu anderen Abteilungen
interest on the trust fund	Zinsertrag aus der Anlage
interfer	beeinträchtigen
Internal Audit	betriebsinterne Kontrollstell
International Relations	internationale Beziehungen bezogen auf Patienten
i. e. = id est	zum Beispiel
internship	Praktikum
intrinsic dignity	inhärente Würde
introduction	Einführung
involved	beteiligt
involving your case	ihren Fall betreffend
is handed to	wird ausgegeben
is least	ist am geringsten
issuance	Herausgabe
issues	Aspekte
it does happen	es kommt vor
it is worth while	es lohnt sich
itemized and detailed explanation	dezidierte und detaillierte Erklärung

job description . . . . Tätigkeitsbeschreibung
job offers. . . . . Stellenangebote
job performance evaluation. . . . . Arbeitsleistungsbewertung
job proficiency . . . . Arbeitskompetenz/-leistung
joint replacement . . . . Gelenkersatz
judiciously. . . . . wachsam
justice . . . . Gerechtigkeit

knowledge and skills . . . . Wissen und Fähigkeiten
knowledge . . . . Wissen

lay term . . . . Laiensprache
learning environment . . . . Lernumfeld
least expensive . . . . am preiswertesten
lecture catalog. . . . . Vorlesungsverzeichnis
legal background. . . . . rechtlicher Hintergrund
legal mandate . . . . gesetzlicher Auftrag
legal proceedings. . . . . rechtliche Verfahren
legal requirements. . . . . rechtliche Vorgaben
legally authorized representative . . . . rechtlich autorisierter Vertreter
legally authorized . . . . rechtlich autorisiert
legally enacted . . . . rechtlich festgelegt
legally incorporated. rechtlich eingeordnet
legislation . . . . Gesetzgebung
letter of recommendation . . . . Empfehlungsschreiben
liberal arts. . . . . Geisteswissenschaften
licence. . . . . Lizenz
licencing exams. . . . . Staatsexamen
licensing and accrediting agencies. . . . . Zulassungs- und Anerkennungsbehörden
life threatening . . . . lebensbedrohlich
line manager. . . . . Fachvorgesetzte
living will . . . . Patientenerklärung
long range objectives. . . . . Langzeitziele
long term . . . . über längere Zeit
LPNs = Licenced Practical Nurses . . . . Schwesternhelferinnen

main duties. . . . . Hauptaufgaben
main goal . . . . Hauptziel
maintain . . . . erhalten
maintenance . . . . Erhaltung
majority . . . . Mehrheit
management training . . . . Managementausbildung
mandatory contributions. . . . . Pflichtbeiträge
manual . . . . Handbuch
marketing and public relations . . . . Vermarktung und Öffentlichkeitsarbeit
Master Degree . . . . 2. Universitätsgrad
Masters Degree in education . . . . Mastergrad in Erziehungswissenschaften
matters . . . . Angelegenheiten

maximum of the salary range .... höchste Gehaltsstufe in einer bestimmten Gehaltskategorie
meal .... Essen
meaning .... Bedeutung
measurable .... messbar
medical bill......................... Krankenhausrechnung
medical ethics commission .... medizinische Ethik-Kommission
medical history...................... Krankheitsgeschichte
medical house staff.................. angestellte Ärzte
medical media........................ medizinische Medien, z. B. Fotolabor
medical office building .... Gebäude mit Arztpraxen, Gesundheitsdiensten
medical orders .... Verordnungen
medical progress notes .... Behandlungsergebnisse/-pläne
medical record .... Patientenakte
medical records...................... Archiv für Krankenakten
medical residents in training........ Ärzte in Ausbildung
medical school clinical practice plans ...... klinische Praxispläne in der medizinischen Ausbildung
medical staff administration .... Management/Betreuung der Belegärzte
medical staff........................ Ärzteschaft
medical staff records................ Ärztliche Dokumentation
medically indicated.................. medizinisch notwendig
medically significant................ medizinisch bedeutende
medicare assignment rate-Medicare .... Kostenerstattungsrate
medication administration .... Arzneimittelvergabe
medication errors .... Fehler bei Arzneimittelvergabe
medications .... Arzneimittel
meet .... erreichen/erfüllen
membership .... Mitgliedschaft
members.............................. Mitglieder
merchant-seamen .... Handelsmarine
merger .... Zusammenschluss
merit................................ Verdienst
met.................................. erfüllt
midwife .... Hebamme
mining .... Bergbau
ministry .... Dienstleistung
misconduct........................... Fehlverhalten
mission statement.................... Aussage zur Aufgabe
mission.............................. Aufgabe
mistake.............................. Fehler
monetary increase.................... Gehaltserhöhung
monetary reward...................... monetäre Anerkennung
monthly premiums .... monatliche Beiträge
moral issues .... moralische Aspekte
must be met .... müssen erfüllt werden
mutual benefit....................... wechselseitiger Nutzen

name tag . . . . Namensschild
national origin . . . . nationale Herkunft
nationwide . . . . landesweit
native . . . . einheimisch
natural science . . . . Naturwissenschaften
needs . . . . Bedürfnisse
night stand . . . . Nachtkästchen
noise abatement . . . . Lärmbeseitigung
nominal . . . . minimal
non-compliance . . . . Mitarbeitsverweigerung
nonfederal. . . . . nichtstaatlich
non-preferred . . . . unbekannter Markenname
notary public. . . . . Notar
noteworthy . . . . erwähnenswert
numerous . . . . zahlreich
nurse call . . . . Rufanlage
nurse recruiter. . . . . Kr.Schwester zuständig für Anwerbung von Pflegepersonal
nurse-run . . . . von Krankenschwestern geführt
nurses notes . . . . Pflegedokumentation
nursing administration . . . . Pflegemenagement
nursing assistants . . . . ungelernte Helferinnen
nursing care needs. . . . . Pflegebedürfnisse
nursing care programs. . . . . Pflegeprogramme
nursing care . . . . Pflege
nursing certificates . . . . pflegerische Staatsexamen
nursing devision's performance . . . . Leistungen des Pflegedienstes
nursing education . . . . innerbetriebliche Fortbildung/ pflegerische Bildung
nursing floors . . . . Pflegestationen
nursing judgements. . . . . pflegerische Entscheidungen
nursing notes . . . . Pflegebericht
nursing personnel . . . . Pflegepersonal
nursing practice . . . . Pflegearbeit
nursing school pins . . . . Schulbrosche
nursing science . . . . Pflegewissenschaft
nursing services. . . . . Pflegedienst
nursing shortage . . . . Schwesternmangel
nursing station . . . . Stationszimmer/Pflegestützpunkt
nursing supervisor. . . . . Abteilungsleitung
nursing task . . . . pflegerische Aufgabe
nursing unit/nursing floor. . . . . Pflegestation
nursing unit . . . . Station
nutritional requirements . . . . Ernährungsbedürfnisse
nutrition . . . . Ernährung

objectives . . . . Ziele
observance . . . . Einhaltung

occasionally. . . . . gelegentlich
off the floor . . . . weg von der Station
officially connected . . . . offiziell verbunden
on account of professional regulations. . . . . . aufgrund professioneller Vorschriften
on account of . . . . aufgrund von
on account . . . . basierend auf
on par. . . . . gleichwertig
on-call time . . . . Bereitschaftsdienst
once accredited . . . . einmal anerkannt
ongoing . . . . fortlaufend
open elective. . . . . Wahlfächer
operation of the Hospital . . . . Krankenhausbetrieb
opportunity. . . . . Gelegenheit
order summary . . . . Verordnungsübersicht
ordered . . . . verordnet
orientation classes. . . . . Einführungskurse
orientation period . . . . Einführungszeit
orientation . . . . Einführung
orthotics . . . . Stützhilfen/Korsette
outcome criteria . . . . Ergebniskriterien
overall organization. Dachorganisation
overall picture . . . . Gesamtbild
overall proficiency. . . . . Gesamtfähigkeiten
overall responsibility . . . . Gesamtverantwortung
overall. . . . . gesamt
overlap . . . . Überschneidung
overtime . . . . Überstunden
overview . . . . Überblick
own funds. . . . . Eigenbeteiligung
ownership . . . . Besitz

paid employment . . . . bezahlte Arbeitszeit
paid holidays. . . . . bezahlte Feiertage
paid hours. . . . . bezahlte Stunden
paid time off. . . . . bezahlte Freizeit
part time. . . . . Teilzeit
partially covered . . . . teilweise abgedeckt
partial. . . . . teilweise
particular event. . . . . spezieller Anlass
particular facility. . . . . bestimmte Einrichtung
particular sequence . . . . bestimmte Reihenfolge
particular . . . . speziell
past illnesses . . . . frühere Erkrankungen
patient accounts . . . . Patienten Konten
patient admission . . . . Patientenaufnahme
patient area. . . . . Patientenbereich
patient care delivery systems . . . . Pflegesysteme
patient care. . . . . Patientenversorgung

patient education . . . . patientenbezogene Gesundheitserziehung
patient library . . . . Patientenbibliothek
patient mix . . . . Patienten mit unterschiedlichen Krankheitsschweregraden
patient services Administration. . . . . Patientenversorgung Management
patient services . . . . Patientenversorgung
patient transfer . . . . Verlegung
patient's stay . . . . Verweildauer
patient-population . . . . Patientengruppe
pay days . . . . Zahltage
pay periods . . . . Gehaltsperiode
pay scale parameters . . . . Gehaltstufen
pay scale . . . . Gehaltsstufen
payment . . . . Zahlung
payroll taxes . . . . Einkommensteuer
pension payments . . . . Pensionsauszahlungen
pension plan . . . . Pensionsplan
performance evaluation. . . . . Leistungsbewertung
performance . . . . Leistung
permission . . . . Erlaubnis
personal conduct. . . . . persönliches Verhalten
personal dignity . . . . persönliche Würde
personal file . . . . Personalakte
personnel . . . . Mitarbeiter
pertaining. . . . . bezüglich
pertinent data . . . . fallbezogene Unterlagen
pertinent. . . . . bedeutend
petition. . . . . Antrag
philosophy . . . . Leitlinie
physical examination. . . . . körperliche Untersuchung
physician relations. Beziehung zu Ärzten
physician services . . . . ärztliche Versorgung
physician statement. . . . . ärztliches Attest
physician's office . . . . Arztpraxis
physician's order sheet. . . . . ärztliches Verordnungsformular
physician's order . . . . ärztliche Verordnungen
physician's progress notes . . . . Ärztliche Dokumentation des Krankheitsverlaufs
physician. . . . . Arzt
plan of treatment . . . . Behandlungsplan
planning and programm development. . . . . . Planung und Entwicklung von Service Programmen
plaque. . . . . Plakette
policies and procedures . . . . Leitlinien und Standards
policy . . . . Leitlinie
position description . . . . Tätigkeitsbeschreibung
possession. . . . . Besitz
postgraduate . . . . nach Grundausbildung

practical experience . . . . pracktische Erfahrung
practices . . . . Arbeitsweisen
practitioner primarily responsible . . . . primär verantwortliche Arzt
practitioner responsible. . . . . verantwortlicher Arzt
practitioner's orders. . . . . ärztliche Verordnungen
practitioner . . . . professionelle Person
precautionary measure . . . . Vorsichtsmaßnahm
predominant . . . . vorherrschend
preferred brand name . . . . bekannter Markenname
preferred provider . . . . bevorzugter Leistungserbringer
pregnant women . . . . schwangere Frauen
premiums . . . . Beiträge
prepaid fees. . . . . im voraus gezahlte Beiträge
preparation . . . . Vorbereitung
prerequisite courses. vorab erforderliche Kurse
prerequisits . . . . Vorleistungen
presence . . . . Anwesenheit
present complaints . . . . derzeitige Beschwerden
present . . . . anwesend
prevailing idea. . . . . vorherrschende Meinung
prevailing . . . . vorherrschend
previous nursing studies . . . . vorhergegangene Pflegestudien
primarily responsible. . . . . primär verantwortlich
prior to departure . . . . vor Abreise
prior to . . . . bevor
privacy . . . . Privatheit
private attending physicians . . . . privat behandelnde Ärzte
private practitioners . . . . privat Praktizierende
privileges. . . . . Rechte
probability of success . . . . Wahrscheinlichkeit des Erfolgs
procedures . . . . Methoden/Untersuchungen
professional growth. professionelles Wachsen
professional regulations. . . . . professionelle Vorgaben
proficient . . . . fähig
progress or regress. . . . . Besserung oder Verschlechterung
progression . . . . Hinführung
promotion of career ladders . . . . Förderung von Karriereleitern
promotion. . . . . (Be-)förderung
prompt response . . . . umgehende Antwort
prompt . . . . umgehend
proof. . . . . Beleg
proper terminology. . . . . richtige Wortwahl
proper. . . . . genau
property . . . . Eigentum
propose to engage. . . . . vorschlagen teilzunehmen
proprietary . . . . in Privatbesitz
prosthetics . . . . Prothesen
protection . . . . Schutz

protective privacy . . . . Isolierung
provided . . . . vorausgesetzt
provider . . . . Leistungserbringer
provides leadership . . . . übernimmt die Führung
providing service . . . . Leistungen erbringen
provision of appropriate care . . . . Erbringung angemessener Behandlung
provision . . . . Verfügbarmachung
public awareness . . . . das öffentliche Bewusstsein
public health agencies . . . . öffentliche Gesundheitsorganisationen
public insurance . . . . staatliche Versicherung
publicly financed . . . . staatlich finanziert
public . . . . öffentlich
purpose . . . . Zweck
pursuit . . . . Bestreben

questionable validity . . . . fragwürdige Richtigkeit
questionnaires . . . . Fragebogen

race . . . . Rasse
ramp . . . . Auffahrt
readily available . . . . leicht verfügbar
reasonable estimate of charges . . . . angemessener Kostenvoranschlag
reasonable expenses . . . . angemessene Kosten
reasonable notice . . . . angemessene Benachrichtigung
reasonable privacy . . . . angemessene Privatheit
reasonably informed participation . . . . angemessen informierter Teilnahme
reason . . . . Ursache
recently . . . . vor kurzem
re-certification . . . . erneute Zertifizierung
recognition . . . . Anerkennung
recommendations . . . . Empfehlungen
records . . . . Befunde
recovery . . . . Wiederherstellung
recruitment and retention . . . . Personalgewinnung und -erhalt
recuperation . . . . Gesundung
reduction . . . . Absenkung
reference service . . . . Nachschlagdienste
referral services . . . . Überweisungsdienste
referrals . . . . Überweisungen
refusal . . . . Verweigerung
regarding policy and programs . . . . bezüglich (Krankenhaus-)Zielsetzung und Programmen
regarding . . . . hinsichtlich
regardless of the source of payment . . . . ungeachtet des Kostenträgers
regardless . . . . ungeachtet
registered nurse . . . . in das professionnelle Register eingetragene Krankenschwester
registration . . . . Registrierung

regulation . . . . Vorschrift
reimbursement . . . . Kostenerstattung
relationship. . . . . Beziehung/Verhältnis
relations . . . . Verhältnis
relative . . . . im Verhältnis
relatives. . . . . Angehörige
reliability. . . . . Verlässlichkeit
rely . . . . sich verlassen
reports . . . . Berichte
representative . . . . stellvertretend
reprimands . . . . Beanstandungen
request . . . . Anfrage
required . . . . erforderlich
requirements. . . . . Anforderungen
research purposes . . . . Forschungszwecke, voluntary freiwillig
research/educational projects. . . . . Forschungs-/Ausbildungsprojekte
research. . . . . Forschung
reserved . . . . vorbehalten
resolution . . . . Bearbeitung
respirators. . . . . Beatmungsapparate
response to care . . . . Auswirkung von Pflege
responses . . . . Reaktionen
responsibility. . . . . Verantwortung
restauration. . . . . Wiederherstellung
restraints. . . . . Sicherungsgurte
restraint . . . . Zurückhaltung
result. . . . . Ergebnis
resuscitation . . . . Reanimation
retaliation . . . . Racheakt
retirement. . . . . Ruhestand
reverence for life . . . . Achtung vor dem Leben
review. . . . . Überprüfung
revision. . . . . Überarbeitung
role models . . . . Rollenvorbilder,
rotating shifts . . . . Schichtdienst
rules and regulations. . . . . Regeln und Vorschriften
rumor line. . . . . Gerüchteküche
running. . . . . Durchführung
rural . . . . ländlich

safety clasps . . . . Sicherheitsverschluss
safety measures . . . . Sicherheitsmaßnahmen
safety services . . . . Sicherheitsdienst
safety systems . . . . Sicherheitssysteme
safety . . . . Sicherheit
salaried . . . . angestellt
salary adjustment . . . . Gehaltserhöhung
salary . . . . Gehalt

samaritans. . . . . ehrenamtliche Helfer
sample . . . . Muster
satisfaction . . . . Zufriedenheit
satisfactory completion . . . . erfolgreicher Abschluss
scale . . . . Stufe
scope of action . . . . Aktionsbereich
scope of work . . . . Arbeitsaufgaben
secure . . . . sicher
security officer . . . . Wachmann
security services . . . . Sicherheitsdienste
selected. . . . . ausgewählt
selection . . . . Auswahl
self-development . . . . Selbstentwicklung
self-employment. . . . . Selbstständigkeit
self-limited . . . . selbst beschränkt
semester break . . . . Semesterferien
senior management position . . . . gehobener Management Position
serious side effects. ernsthafte Nebenwirkungen
serious . . . . ernsthaft
seriousness of purpose. . . . . Ernsthaftigkeit für ihre Aufgaben
services rendered. . . . . erbrachte Leistungen
set forth . . . . festgelegt
several. . . . . mehrere
shift differential . . . . Schichtzulage
shifts. . . . . Arbeitsschichten
short-term . . . . kurzeitig
should be communicated . . . . sollte mitgeteilt werden
show proof . . . . belegen
sick time. . . . . Krankheitstage
similar. . . . . ähnlich
sitting on a jury. . . . . Schöffendienste
situated. . . . . eingebettet
skilled care facilities . . . . Einrichtungen mit professionellem Pflegedienst
skilled nursing facilities. . . . . Einrichtungen mit professionellem Pflegedienst
skilled nursing . . . . professionelle Pflege
Social Security Service . . . . staatliche Rentenversicherung
sole. . . . . einzig
solely . . . . ausschließlich
someone of your own sex . . . . eine Person des eigenen Geschlechts
sources of payment . . . . Bezahlungsmodus
sources . . . . Mittel
special areas . . . . Spezialeinheiten
special occasions . . . . besondere Anlässe
specialty area. . . . . Funktionsbereich
specialty practice. . . . . fachspezifische Pflegepraxis
specific matters . . . . bestimmte Punkte

spiritual values . . . . geistige Werte
spouses . . . . Ehegatten
staff development . . . . Personalentwicklung
staff performance appraisal . . . . Mitarbeiterbewertung
staffed. . . . . mit Personal besetzt
staffing . . . . Personalzuteilung
staff . . . . Personal
State Board Examination . . . . Staatsexamen
state board of nursing . . . . Pflegekammer
state boards. . . . . Staatsexamen
state controlling agencies . . . . staatliche Kontrollbehörden
state licensure laws . . . . staatliche Lizenzierungsgesetze
state subsidized. . . . . staatlich subventioniert
state . . . . Bundesstaat
status and salary . . . . Position und Gehalt
stay on good terms . . . . gute Beziehungen unterhalten
stay. . . . . Verweildauer
subjects. . . . . Fächer/Themen
submission of proof. Vorlage des Beweises
subordinate. . . . . Nachgeordnete
subsequently . . . . folglich
success expected . . . . erwarteter Erfolg
successfully passed . . . . erfolgreich bestanden
suction . . . . Saugung
suggestions . . . . Vorschläge
superior. . . . . Vorgesetzter
supervisor . . . . Abteilungsleitung
supplement . . . . Ergänzung
support departments. . . . . unterstützende Abteilungen
support services. . . . . Unterstützungsdienste
support . . . . Unterstützung
surgeons . . . . Chirurgen
surgery . . . . Chirurgie/Operationen/Operations-abteilung
surname . . . . Familienname
surroundings. . . . . Umfeld
survival . . . . Überleben
suspicious . . . . verdächtig
systems approach . . . . systematische Herangehensweise
systems . . . . betriebsinterne Systeme

takes place . . . . ergibt sich
task. . . . . Aufgabe
tax funds. . . . . Steuergelder
tax . . . . Steuer
temporary licensure. . . . . zeitlich begrenzte Lizenz

termination of your eligibility
for reimbursement . . . . vor Ablauf ihres Anspruchs auf Kostenerstattung
the best of your knowledge . . . . nach bestem Wissen
the insured . . . . der Versicherte
the more . . . . je mehr
the passing on . . . . Weitergabe
the patient's response . . . . das Pflegeergebnis
the public at large . . . . Öffentlichkeit
the way . . . . die Art und Weise
theft . . . . Diebstahl
therapists on staff . . . . angestellte Therapeuten
third party payment . . . . Krankenversicherungen
third party payor . . . . Versicherung
thorough knowledge . . . . gündliche Kenntnisse
those who are served . . . . diejenigen, die bedient werden/ Leistungsempfänger
those who are serving . . . . diejenigen, die dienen/Leistungserbringer
thus . . . . auf diese Weise
time frame . . . . zeitlicher Rahmen
time of employment . . . . Zeit der Anstellung
time schedule . . . . Dienstplan
timely notice . . . . rechtzeitige Benachrichtigung
to accelerate . . . . beschleunigen
to accept . . . . annehmen
to accompany . . . . begleiten
to accomplish a certain task . . . . eine bestimmte Tätigkeit durchführen
to accord . . . . bewilligen
to achieve . . . . erreichen
to actively subscribe . . . . aktive mittragen
to add . . . . beitragen
to address . . . . ansprechen
to adhere . . . . festhalten
to adjoin . . . . anschließen
to adjust . . . . anpassen
to administer . . . . durchführen/verwalten
to admit . . . . aufnehmen
to advance . . . . fortschreiten/vorwärts bringen
to affect . . . . betreffen
to affirm . . . . bekräftigen
to agree . . . . übereinstimmen
to aim . . . . abzielen
to allow . . . . erlauben
to announce . . . . ausrufen
to appear . . . . erscheinen
to apply . . . . beantragen/anwenden/gelten/einsetzen
to approach . . . . herantreten
to approve . . . . genehmigen

to ascertain . . . . sicherstellen
to assess . . . . einschätzen
to assign . . . . zuteilen
to assist. . . . . mithelfen/unterstützen
to assume responsibility . . . . Verantwortung übernehmen
to assure . . . . versichern
to attach . . . . anbringen
to attain . . . . erreichen
to attend to. . . . . behandeln/befasst sein/teilnehmen
to avoid. . . . . vermeiden
to await. . . . . erwarten
to be committed . . . . verpflichtet sein
to be considerate. . . . . rücksichtsvoll sein
to be dedicated . . . . verpflichtet sein
to be fortified . . . . gestärkt sein
to be in charge . . . . verantwortlich sein
to be involved . . . . befasst sein
to be present. . . . . anwesend sein
to be proficient . . . . fähig/fließend sein
to be responsible. . . . . verantwortlich sein
to be subjected to . . . . ausgesetzt sein
to be subjected . . . . unterzogen werden
to believe . . . . glauben
to benefit . . . . profitieren
to bestow . . . . verleihen
to call . . . . nennen
to carry out. . . . . durchführen
to certify. . . . . bestätigen
to chart. . . . . dokumentieren
to chose . . . . auswählen
to cite . . . . aufzeigen
to clarify expectations . . . . Erwartungen klären
to combine . . . . zusammenlegen
to commend . . . . loben
to compare . . . . vergleichen
to compile. . . . . zusammenfügen
to complain. . . . . sich beschweren
to complete. . . . . abschließen
to comply . . . . sich daran halten
to comprehend . . . . verstehen
to compromise . . . . beeinträchtigen
to conduct descreetly. . . . . vertraulich führen
to conduct. . . . . durchführen
to confer . . . . besprechen
to consider . . . . betrachten
to consist of . . . . bestehend aus
to consistently exemplify. . . . . beständig verkörpern
to consult . . . . konsultieren

to contain . . . . enthalten
to contract . . . . vertraglich festlegen
to contribute. . . . . beitragen
to convey . . . . vermitteln
to cope . . . . bewältigen
to cover. . . . . abdecken
to deal with. . . . . behandeln/sich befassen
to declare . . . . festlegen/erklären
to decrease . . . . absenken
to dedicate . . . . sich für etwas einsetzen
to deem. . . . . erachten
to delineate. . . . . skizzieren
to deliver. . . . . durchführen
to demonstrate . . . . zeigen
to demote . . . . zurückstufen
to depend . . . . abhängig sein
to deposit . . . . einzahlen
to derive . . . . ableiten
to describe . . . . beschreiben
to design. . . . . erstellen
to desire . . . . wünschen
to determine . . . . bestimmen/feststellen
to develop. . . . . entwickeln
to differentiate . . . . unterscheiden
to differ. . . . . unterschiedlich sein
to discuss . . . . besprechen
to dispel . . . . zerstreuen
to display . . . . ausstellen
to disrupt . . . . unterbrechen
to diversify . . . . differenzieren
to divide . . . . einteilen
to earn . . . . erwerben
to elect . . . . wählen
to eliminate. . . . . aufarbeiten/beheben
to emphasize. . . . . betonen
to employ . . . . beschäftigen
to empower. . . . . befähigen
to enable. . . . . befähigen
to encourage . . . . ermuntern
to endeaver . . . . sich bemühen
to endow. . . . . übergeben
to enforce . . . . durchsetzen
to enhance . . . . fördern
to ensure. . . . . sicherstellen
to entail . . . . nach sich ziehen
to entitle. . . . . berechtigen
to equip . . . . ausstatten
to establish objectives . . . . Ziele setzen

to establish .... festlegen
to evolve .... herausbilden
to examplify .... verdeutlichen
to execute .... durchführen
to expand .... erweitern
to expect .... erwarten
to experience......................... erleben
to express .... ausdrücken
to facilitate .... erleichtern
to fail .... durchfallen
to familiarize........................ bekanntmachen
to file a grievance .... eine Beschwerde einreichen
to file .... ablegen
to fine tune .... differenzieren
to foster .... hegen
to found .... gründen
to fulfil .... erfüllen
to fulfill............................ erfüllen
to gather .... sammeln
to guard .... darüber wachen
to happen .... vorkommen
to head .... leiten
to include .... miteinbeziehen/einschließen
to incorporate .... integrieren
to indicate........................... anzeigen
to initiate .... beginnen
to integrate .... einfügen
to introduce .... vorstellen
to issue .... herausgeben
to label .... beschriften
to lecture............................ lehren
to licence .... genehmigen
to make known .... bekannt machen
to meet .... erfüllen
to modify .... überarbeiten
to monitor .... überwachen
to negotiate.......................... verhandeln
to notify .... benachrichtigen
to observe .... beobachten
to obtain .... erwerben/erhalten
to occur.............................. erscheinen/auftreten
to offer .... anbieten
to opt .... entscheiden
to order.............................. verordnen
to pass on .... weiterleiten
to pass successfully .... erfolgreich bestehen
to pass............................... bestehen
to perceive .... wahrnehmen

to perform . . . . durchführen
to pertain to . . . . zugehören
to pertain . . . . zugehören
to possess . . . . besitzen
to prepare in advance . . . . im vorhinein vorbereiten
to prepare . . . . vorbereiten
to preserve . . . . bewahren
to prevent . . . . verhindern
to procure . . . . beschaffen
to produce. . . . . erzeugen
to proliferate. . . . . ausbreiten
to prolong. . . . . verlängern
to promote . . . . fördern
to proof. . . . . belegen
to propose. . . . . vorschlagen
to provide means. . . . . Mittel einsetzen
to provide services. verfügbar machen von Diensten
to provide . . . . zur Verfügung stellen
to purchase . . . . kaufen
to reach. . . . . erreichen
to realize. . . . . wahrnehmen
to receive . . . . erhalten
to recognize . . . . anerkennen
to recommend. . . . . empfehlen
to recruit. . . . . anheuern
to reduce. . . . . herabsetzen
to refer . . . . verweisen
to refine . . . . verfeinern
to reflect . . . . widerspiegeln
to refuse treatment . . . . Behandlung verweigern
to refuse . . . . ablehnen/verweigern
to register a complaint . . . . eine Beschwerde vorbringen
to register . . . . einschreiben
to remain . . . . verbleiben
to render care . . . . pflegen
to renew . . . . erneuern
to repeat . . . . wiederholen
to report . . . . berichten
to represent. . . . . vertreten
to request . . . . anfordern
to require . . . . (er)fordern
to reserve the right . . . . sich vorbehalten
to resolve . . . . lösen
to retire. . . . . in Rente gehen
to review. . . . . überprüfen
to revise . . . . überarbeiten
to safeguard . . . . beschützen
to satisfy . . . . befriedigen

to schedule . . . . festlegen/einteilen
to see to it. . . . . darauf achten
to seek . . . . danach streben/suchen
to select . . . . auswählen
to serve. . . . . dienen
to shape . . . . bestimmen
to shoulder responsibility . . . . Verantwortung tragen
to show proof . . . . belegen
to signify. . . . . zeigen
to sign. . . . . unterschreiben
to single out . . . . hervorheben
to solve . . . . lösen
to state . . . . angeben
to strife for . . . . danach streben
to strive. . . . . sich bemühen
to submit . . . . vorlegen
to suggest . . . . vorschlagen
to supervise. . . . . beaufsichtigen
to support. . . . . unterstützen
to tailor to. . . . . zuschneiden
to take care of . . . . betreuen
to take into consideration . . . . berücksichtigen
to terminate . . . . auflösen
to treat . . . . behandeln
to update . . . . aktualisieren
to utilize . . . . einsetzen
to verify . . . . beglaubigen
to view . . . . betrachten
to withdraw . . . . entziehen
topics . . . . Themen
tracks . . . . Richtungen
trajectory . . . . Krankheitsverlauf
transfer . . . . Verlegung/Wechsel (der Arbeitsstelle)
treatment options . . . . Behandlungsmöglichkeiten
treatment . . . . Behandlung
tripartite . . . . dreiteilig
tuition reimbursement . . . . Studiengebührenerstattung
tuition. . . . . Studiengebühren

understanding consent . . . . verstehende Einwilligung
unencumbered . . . . unbelastet
unexpected changes in your condition. . . . . . unerwartete Veränderungen Ihres Zustandes
unfamiliar . . . . unbekannt
unfoldings. . . . . Entfaltungen
uniform code . . . . Arbeitskleidungsvorschrift
unions. . . . . Gewerkschaften
unique . . . . einmalig
uniqueness . . . . Einmaligkeit

unit . . . . Station
university of applied sciences . . . . Fachhochschule
unjust . . . . ungerecht
unreasonably disturbing . . . . unzumutbar störend
unrestricted . . . . ungemindert
unspecific terms . . . . allgemeine Anreden
unusual . . . . ungewöhnlich
upon request . . . . auf Anforderung
urban . . . . städtisch
usual . . . . üblich
utilization . . . . Einsatz

vacation . . . . Urlaub
valid . . . . gültig
validity of licensures . . . . Gültigkeit der Berufserlaubnis
valuables . . . . Wertsachen
value-based . . . . auf ideellen Werten basierend
values . . . . Werte
variations in coverage . . . . Unterschiede in der Abdeckung
variety of avenues . . . . unterschiedliche Weise
variety . . . . Vielfalt
various . . . . vielseitig
visiting nurse association . . . . häusliche Pflege
vital signs . . . . vitale Zeichen
vocational or trade schools . . . . Berufsfachschulen
vocation . . . . Beruf
voluntary participation . . . . freiwillige Teilnahme
voluntary review . . . . freiwillige Überprüfung
voluntary . . . . freiwillig
volunteers . . . . ehrenamtliche Helfer/innen

wage and salary administration . . . . Lohn und Gehaltpolitik
wall outlets . . . . Wandanschlüsse
welcome note . . . . Willkommensgruß
welfare . . . . Wohlergehen
well child . . . . gesundes Kind
well taken care of . . . . gut betreut
wheel chair . . . . Rolls
wide range . . . . großer Bereich
wide scope . . . . breite Basis
within the assigned pay grade . . . . innerhalb der festgelegten Gehaltsgrenzen
within the parameters . . . . innerhalb der Grenzen
witness . . . . Zeuge
word-processing . . . . Computerabteilung
work environment . . . . Arbeitsumfeld
work habits . . . . Arbeitsgewohnheiten
work performance . . . . Arbeitsleeistung
work permit . . . . Arbeitserlaubnis

work related . . . . arbeitsbezogen
work uniforms . . . . Arbeitskleidung
worth and importance. . . . . Wert und Bedeutung
written orders . . . . schriftliche Verordnungen

X-Ray. . . . . Röntgenabteilung/-aufnahme/röntgen

years of service . . . . Arbeitsjahre
you can reasonably be expected
to understand. . . . . beim dem ein Verständnis Ihrerseits vorausgesetzt werden kann
your own request. . . . . eigene Anforderung